WHAT'S THE POINT
OF COLLEGE?

WHAT'S THE POINT OF COLLEGE?

Seeking Purpose in an Age of Reform

JOHANN N. NEEM

JOHNS HOPKINS UNIVERSITY PRESS

Baltimore

© 2019 Johns Hopkins University Press
All rights reserved. Published 2019
Printed in the United States of America on acid-free paper
9 8 7 6 5 4 3 2 1

Johns Hopkins University Press
2715 North Charles Street
Baltimore, Maryland 21218-4363
www.press.jhu.edu

Library of Congress Cataloging-in-Publication Data

Names: Neem, Johann N., 1974– author.
Title: What's the point of college? : seeking purpose in an age of reform /
  Johann N. Neem.
Description: Baltimore : Johns Hopkins University Press, 2019. | Includes
  bibliographical references and index.
Identifiers: LCCN 2018051293 | ISBN 9781421429885 (acid-free paper) |
  ISBN 9781421429892 (electronic) | ISBN 1421429888 (acid-free paper) |
  ISBN 1421429896 (electronic)
Subjects: LCSH: Education, Higher—Aims and objectives--United States. |
  Universities and colleges—United States. | Educational change—United
  States.
Classification: LCC LA227.4 .N43 2019 | DDC 378/.01—dc23
LC record available at https://lccn.loc.gov/2018051293

A catalog record for this book is available from the British Library.

*Special discounts are available for bulk purchases of this book. For more information,
please contact Special Sales at 410-516-6936 or specialsales@press.jhu.edu.*

Johns Hopkins University Press uses environmentally friendly book materials,
including recycled text paper that is composed of at least 30 percent
post-consumer waste, whenever possible.

For my students—past, present, and future

The collegiate course of study . . . may be carefully distinguished from several *other* objects and plans, with which it has been too often confounded. It is far from embracing *every thing* which the student will ever have occasion to learn. The object is not to *finish* his education; but to lay the foundation, and to advance as far in rearing the superstructure, as the short period of his residence here will admit. If he acquires here a thorough knowledge of the principles of science, he may then, in a great measure, educate himself. He has, at least, been taught *how* to learn. With the aid of books, and means of observation, he may be constantly advancing in knowledge.

—*Reports on the Course of Instruction in Yale College by a Committee of the Corporation* (1828)

Today's college graduate may have gained technical or professional training in one field of work or another, but is only incidentally, if at all, made ready for performing his duties as a man, a parent, and a citizen. Too often he is "educated" in that he has acquired competence in some particular occupation, yet falls short of that human wholeness and civic conscience which the cooperative activities of citizenship require.

—*Higher Education for American Democracy.* A Report of the President's Commission on Higher Education (1947)

America's national capacity for excellence, innovation and leadership in higher education will be central to our ability to sustain economic growth and social cohesiveness. Our colleges and universities will be a key source of the human and intellectual capital needed to increase workforce productivity and growth. They must also continue to be the major route for new generations of Americans to achieve social mobility.

—*A Test of Leadership: Charting the Future of U.S. Higher Education.* A Report of the Commission Appointed by Secretary of Education Margaret Spellings (2006)

CONTENTS

SCHOLARSHIP

On Education versus Degrees

IT HIT me one day in class: after reading contradictory reports on the relationship between college majors and future salaries, one of my students almost burst into tears. I asked her what was wrong. She was just overwhelmed, as were, I soon realized, other students in my class. It just didn't make sense to them. One study argued that students should choose STEM and vocational majors; the other concluded that the liberal arts are the best ticket to successful careers and good salaries. Which was correct?

There is intense pressure today to increase the number of Americans with college degrees. Because college degrees are correlated with all kinds of good effects—higher salaries for graduates, greater personal happiness, lower crime rates, highly skilled workers—policy makers from both parties have pushed to increase access, but because college is expensive, they also want to find ways to get more Americans in and out of college cheaply and quickly. As a result, we tend to spend more time thinking about how to increase the number of degrees than about what kind of education a college should offer.

My students feel this pressure. They have been told that their only chance at future success is to get a college degree, and absent better economic and labor policies, who can blame them for listening? They arrive on campus believing—rightly or wrongly—that the choices that they make now will determine the course of their lives. Whether they want to be in school or not, they feel the weight of the world upon them. I see this in their eyes and hear it in their words.

In the autumn, I often teach a course called Going to College in America, an interdisciplinary exploration of the purposes and functions of college. We draw on economics, history, philosophy, and many other fields to understand college past and present. Many of my students are in the first term of their first year. They are excited and anxious. Although they know that they need to get their degree, they are often unsure about what kind of education they want.

My students attend a public comprehensive university, the kind attended by most four-year college students. Too often, news stories focus on students at the most elite schools—the public flagships or the Ivy League. These schools are not representative of the experiences of most students, nor of most professors. Many of my students are first-generation collegians, and many work to pay their tuition and expenses.

Many of my students come to college because they want to achieve financial security. They are not seeking wealth in some greedy way; indeed, I have been impressed by how many of them want to leave the world a better place. But my students, reasonably, want good jobs. That's the primary reason they are on campus, something that is increasingly true of students nationwide. Yet in my class they learn that the purposes of college education have historically been civic and intellectual, not just vocational. They discover that the liberal arts and sciences, which were once the entire curriculum, are today being pushed to the margins of the university. They also experience some whiplash. They come for degrees and want to choose so-called practical majors, but their first year is spent largely in general education courses in the arts and sciences. Many don't even know what a liberal education is, much less what it's for. It feels wasteful. They wonder whether it will pay off.

Their concerns are shared and shaped by the words of policy makers who proclaim that the traditional liberal purposes of college education are indeed wasteful. We need useful degrees, so many of our leaders proclaim, implying that degrees in the arts and sciences are not useful. Some are more explicit, mocking students who choose to major in the traditional academic disciplines. Policy makers from both parties now see the purpose of college primarily as job training. In our quest to expand access to *degrees*, we have lost sight of what should define a good college *education*.

One can get a sense of how lost we are by looking at one moment in the recent past. In 2015, the Obama administration released the much-awaited, much-debated College Scorecard (available at https://collegescorecard .ed.gov/). For the first time, the US Department of Education would offer Americans a guide to compare colleges and universities. The Scorecard sought to help Americans make sense of the complicated and difficult terrain of choosing a college. Further, it sought to protect Americans from colleges—especially for-profit ones—that made big promises but failed to deliver. But the Scorecard also supported the administration's broader effort to redefine the purpose of higher education as the preparation of young Americans for high-paying jobs. As president, Barack Obama mocked art history majors and argued that today's "knowledge economy" requires that colleges and universities emulate those institutions in countries that are "spending less time teaching things that don't matter and more time teaching things that do."[1]

Many states have pursued similar paths. Across the country, governors have pushed public colleges and universities to publicize graduates' salaries in the hope that this information will guide students' choices and, in turn, pressure colleges to focus on those degrees that lead to the highest-paying jobs. Many have also sought alternative programs, often online, to allow students to finish their degrees as fast as they can instead of spending four years devoted to full-time study.

The clear implication of these policies is that the

point of a college degree is to get in and out as cheaply and quickly as possible in order to secure a job with a big salary. But do we want to measure the quality of a college education by graduates' salaries? A visitor to the federal Scorecard or to state-level websites cannot help but conclude that the quality of an education is reflected in how much graduates make.[2] If the purpose of getting into college is getting out of college, then the College Scorecard offers us good information, but if what happens during one's time in college also matters, it offers us little of value.

Ultimately, the fault of these rankings stems from our not knowing what makes a good college education because we don't agree on what college is for. We have permitted our colleges to become curricular food courts, serving up degrees in everything from physical therapy or business to philosophy. How does one distinguish among these offerings? How does one judge which is more nutritious? Do we have any criteria?

One answer is that college is not for anything and everything, that there are specific goods that compose a college education. But where would that get us? Nowhere—unless we could agree, at least provisionally, on what those goods are. Is college for creating liberally educated adults? If so, then many of the programs they offer—business is America's largest major (see chapter 6)—are incompatible with a college education. And if college is about liberal education, how do we know whether an institution has been effective? A liberal education, above all, is a phenomenological experience: it is about a *coming to be* over time that is experienced subjectively. It is about reading—and discussing and writing about—specific texts that happen to reshape our perspective about ourselves or the world. It is about how we emerge, after several years spent in institutions devoted to thought, as different people.

How can this complex enterprise be measured? The best we can do, perhaps, is to create assessment tools that make it more likely that more students will have the kinds of intellectual experiences that compose the best college educations. What is the quality of faculty-student interaction? Are most of the faculty tenured? What kind of work do students complete? What percentage of students major in the arts and sciences? What kind of general education program is in place?

How would we know if such a rating would work? Shouldn't we be skeptical about subjective judgments? Perhaps, but we still might ask, What do people do with their lives? How many of them are still reading literature? Do they keep up with the news and subscribe to magazines? How many work in public service? How many go to the theater, or vote, or belong to civic and religious associations? Of course, even the answers to these questions can tell us only so much.

More fundamentally, such measures would be meaningful only if we thought college was a place one attended to gain a liberal education. The diversity of American postsecondary institutions—which range from community colleges that offer both liberal and technical education to schools that emphasize engineering to religious institutions—makes finding common ground difficult. A successful program at a technical school or community college would be, and should be, evaluated by criteria different from what Swarthmore might use.

We could turn to generic measures, such as the Collegiate Learning Assessment, which test abstract skills like critical thinking. The challenge here is that thought can never be abstracted from the material at hand—the facts, the theories, and what a person makes of them (see chapters 7, 9). Yet it is unfair to students and families to offer no guidelines or measures. The collegiate landscape is too confusing. For-profit institutions prey on their customers, offering expensive degrees for people willing to go into a lot of debt.[3] Are they worth it? How to choose? As citizens, we want to know that our money is being well spent, and students want to know that they are making good choices.

Absent any consensus, we Americans chose the lowest common denominator, a measure that perhaps we have no choice but to embrace: How much money will a degree from X or Y lead to? That clearly is what is wrong with the Scorecard, but it may also reflect what's wrong with us. In the end, perhaps we Americans agree about what college is for.

I can't shake the picture of my confused student, on the verge of tears, shaking her head in frustration. Her family, no doubt, had sacrificed to get her there, and she had done everything right to earn a seat in my class. She wanted to know what she had to do now that she was in college. What should I tell her? This book is my effort to explain to her—and to others concerned with the future of America's colleges—what, to me at least, is the answer to that question.

WHAT'S THE POINT
OF COLLEGE?

INTRODUCTION

On the Purpose(s) of College Education

HIGHER EDUCATION is in the news. Are colleges teaching critical thinking? Do graduates have the skills necessary for success in a changing economy? Should we spend taxpayer money on the liberal arts? Is college too expensive? Should we move online? Are the traditional colleges too old-fashioned to change? Reformers from the White House to Wall Street are eager to provide alternatives.

The discussion is often vitriolic, in part because of the intense pressure exerted by internal and external stakeholders and because higher education today includes a diverse array of institutions that are not always distinguished from one another. At a deeper level, however, our disagreements stem from the fact that we speak very different languages, each of which reflects, ultimately, different assumptions about the nature and purpose of collegiate education in America. At its heart, the conversation is about values.

There are three dominant languages that we use to talk about higher education, and each reflects, ultimately, the different values of its advocates. Many administrators, policy makers, and citizens are either *utilitarian* or *pragmatic*. Utilitarians tend to focus on how schools can meet students' preexisting preferences, whereas pragmatists focus more on institutions than on individuals. For them both, the question is how our colleges should evolve to meet the needs of an ever-changing world. In contrast, a large number of faculty members and many administrators, especially in the traditional academic disciplines, emphasize the *virtues* of colleges. To them, there are specific things that a college education stands for, and those things must be protected and cared for, even as students' preferences and the world changes.

Utilitarianism

One of the dominant languages among higher education reformers is utilitarianism, which dates back to British philosopher Jeremy Bentham. In *An Introduction to the Principles of Morals and Legislation* (1789), Bentham defined utility as "that principle which approves or disapproves every action whatsoever, according to the tendency which it appears to have to augment or diminish the happiness of the party whose interest is in question." Happiness is defined by pleasure, unhappiness by pain. Every human being, in Bentham's understanding, seeks to maximize pleasure and avoid pain. Legal and moral "sanctions," like the threat of punishment, work because violating them can cause pain.

As a concept, utility has no content: it does not seek to define happiness as a particular good. It is agnostic. Utilitarianism is a mode of thinking that, without stating what *ought* to cause pleasure, tries to maximize social happiness.

A utilitarian approach to higher education assumes that colleges must be primarily outward-looking, responding to the wishes of higher education's clients. For-profits, in particular, do not seek to change their students' preferences but instead treat their students like customers. Give the students the kinds of programs they want to achieve what they want. The customer, after all, is always right.

That mantra, moreover, has contributed to a broader set of assumptions in traditional colleges. To many reformers and administrators, colleges should offer the kinds of programs students want in the way that they want it to maximize utility. As Jeffrey Selingo writes in *College (Un)Bound*, "colleges are turning into businesses where customers—in this case, students—expect to be satisfied. They have come to regard their professors as service providers."[1]

Utilitarians believe that they are engaged in a noble service: to help students in their own personal pursuit of happiness. At the same time, the utilitarian approach offers no sense of what ought to constitute a college education. It leaves these questions up to the students and the broader marketplace.

Of course, since John Stuart Mill in the nineteenth century, some utilitarians have believed that there are "higher" and "lower" forms of pleasure. Mill argued that we should not consider all preferences equal but, instead, defer to the preferences of the people who are best-informed about what promotes long-term happiness. Yet the utilitarian strain among higher education reformers is not informed by Mill, but by a simpler calculus, in which students' and employers' preferences must be satisfied rather than changed. As Mark Edmundson has written, the modern university seeks "to serve—and not challenge—the students."[2]

Pragmatism

If utilitarians emphasize individual students' desires, pragmatists seek to reform institutions. We recently had, perhaps for the first time, a true pragmatist in the White House. President Barack Obama was committed to a theory of knowledge and politics derived from a revival of ideas that originated among such thinkers as John Dewey.[3] Obama may have been a self-proclaimed pragmatist, but pragmatism is a widely shared philosophy, and it shapes how many Americans think about higher education.

To be clear, pragmatism is not to be confused with practicality. All kinds of people can be practical. Pragmatism, instead, is a particular stance in relation to knowledge and how it works. To pragmatists, the issue is not what is true, but what works. In his famous essay on the "reflex arc" in psychology (1896), Dewey criticized those who distinguished between stimulus and response, noting that each existed in relation to the other. This early insight shaped Dewey's discussion of society. Like the reflex arc, our ideas must exist in constant feedback with changing external realities—our beliefs must change with time. If inherited ideas stop working, they must be changed so that the means we use will bring us the ends we desire.

To Dewey and others of his generation, the scientific temper and the democratic temper were the same thing. Democracies should exhibit a spirit of experimentation, with truth always tested by the results it achieves. If the results are inadequate, then so too are the ideas or the truth. Truth is not derived *a priori* but is a result of constantly testing hypotheses and being willing to revise assumptions. Things will change as society changes. Truth must fit circumstances.

President Obama emphasized these Deweyan elements throughout his tenure. He consistently eschewed loyalty to policies because they were Democratic or Republican, arguing instead that we should "experiment and invest on anything that works."[4] He believed in looking at outcomes alone. In health care, in K–12 education, and in higher education, he wanted data-based decision making. He was less committed to the means used to achieve the outcomes that he desired. For example, Americans could expand access to health care through a universal public system or through expanding the role of for-profit insurance providers. To some, these approaches are fundamentally different. To Obama, on the other hand, the real test was whether more people had affordable health care. He did not ask what was inherently good, but rather what worked.

Obama's pragmatic approach made it hard to distinguish means from ends. In higher education, Obama abandoned any commitment to inherited practices—as his secretary of education Arne Duncan noted, "we need some disruptive innovation in higher education."[5] The president himself promised to "shake up" higher education, and his reform plans touted alternative delivery models.[6]

But how is the end of higher education to be defined? Pragmatists focus on what is needed *today*. They do not look to the past; they are resolutely presentist in their commitments. What is today's world and how does higher education best serve it? There is a Darwinian assumption: if colleges do not adapt to a changing external environment, they will die.

Implicitly, however, there are assumptions that define what counts. For John Dewey, a changing society required changing institutions and practices, but always to serve democracy. But for pragmatic policy makers today, the changing environment is the economy: higher education must adjust to changing *economic* needs; higher education is for jobs.[7] Thus, policy makers from both parties promote a "completion agenda," which seeks, by any means available, to produce more degrees at a cheaper cost. Hence, the White House's College Scorecard, which emphasizes employment and value but not values.[8] And increasingly, states are publishing their own scorecards, which list each major or program, with expected salaries.

Today's pragmatists aspire to transform higher education to fit today's economic context. They are less concerned with colleges' own purposes. Instead, they see the past as a burden, something to be overcome. Indeed, they are not committed to any specific institutions or practices, but instead promote and desire experimentation to achieve their goals—as Obama put it, anything that works.

Virtue Ethics

There is a third way to think about college education, one that takes seriously colleges' own purposes: virtue ethics. Virtue ethics dates back to Aristotle and has been revived recently by philosophers Alasdair MacIntyre and Michael Sandel.[9] To utilitarians, colleges should satisfy the ends desired by students. To pragmatists, both the means and ends change with time; there is no essence that must remain constant. For the virtue ethicist, on the other hand, the ends are fairly constant, as are the means, for the means cannot be separated from the ends. The means are the practices that sustain the virtues of a college—those characteristics that are vital for it to achieve its end.

This book, taking inspiration from MacIntyre and Sandel, examines questions of college reform from the perspective of virtue ethics. It thus offers a distinct vista on such issues as online education, for-profit education, and the relationship between liberal and professional education. It seeks to provide *a way to think about* the questions higher education faces as much as it hopes to offer specific answers to those questions.

The issue is not whether colleges can or should change (of course they should!), or whether professors can or should innovate, but that colleges have a *telos,* or end: to encourage in their students and faculty the ability to acquire and to use knowledge to interpret the world. A college should be a "community of learning."[10] There is, in other words, something about colleges that distinguish them from other kinds of institutions.

Because colleges value the quest for knowledge, they aspire to foster intellectual virtues in all their members— traits such as curiosity, a commitment to truth, and a desire to use knowledge to better oneself and society. This is the distinct way in which colleges serve society and individual students. Unlike other institutions, colleges exist for the intellect. But intellectual virtues are not natural; they have to be cultivated. Developing virtues depends on practicing them. One scholar writes that a virtue is neither a capacity nor a skill but "a state of the soul, that it is acquired, and that it is (at least usually) the result of habituation."[11]

A good college therefore must offer students and professors real, meaningful, and repeated opportunities to engage in the life of the mind. In classrooms and labs and libraries, students and professors must devote their time to seeking insight from the arts and sciences. Only by repetition will the intellectual virtues become internalized. A college graduate should not just have new knowledge and skills; she should be the *kind of person* who strives to use her intellectual skills to seek knowledge to understand the world around her more effectively. A good college education therefore is not just about what one knows or the skills one learns. It is also about character.

One can get a sense of the relationship of virtues and practices to the ends of an institution by comparing colleges to churches. In a church, devotional practices are designed to help reinforce the right beliefs and to orient people to God. Belief is something that develops over time and is internalized through repeated participation in a church's rituals. There is no way, from this perspective, for a church to sustain its ends if the rituals that give them daily life are obliterated.

The same is true for colleges. For them to achieve their telos, they need to be places where students and professors consistently practice the life of the mind. A college graduate should, by virtue of the liberal education he has received, emerge as someone different from who he was before. As in a church, the goal is not just to give all people what they want (as utilitarianism would have it) or to accommodate every worldly need (as some pragmatists suggest) but instead to help students and professors orient their lives around new purposes. The test of a good education is whether a college graduate values the education for itself and not just for the degree. Aristotle considered virtues to be dispositions that are related to the achievement of a good—a good life, a good society. A good college, thus, must cultivate certain virtues or dispositions in both faculty and students.

Implications

Advocates of a virtue ethics–based approach to colleges believe that what they do is useful, even if it is not motivated by utilitarianism, and practical, even if it is not shaped by pragmatism. The questions that must be asked are, Practical and useful for what, for whom, and how? These questions will be answered—and as I make clear in the book, have been answered—very differently by utilitarianism, pragmatism, and by my analysis. A virtue-ethical approach presumes that colleges are useful and practical because of the specific ends they pursue and the practices that sustain those ends. Colleges should ask, How does a meaningful college education produce the habits and virtues of mind that encourage people to make thoughtful assessments of the world that they inhabit, and to use their skills and knowledge to enrich their own lives, our democracy, and the economy?

Professors and college administrators who question the benefits of many higher education reforms are not just sticks-in-the-mud. When they look at for-profit schools, MOOCs (massive open online courses), the shift from the liberal arts and sciences to more vocational degrees, new schools that lack any professors, the growth of adjunct teaching, and the commercialization of research, they do not see a threat primarily to their livelihood but to institutions that cultivate virtues that are unlikely to be preserved if utilitarians or pragmatists have their way.[12] Academics take their inheritance seriously and hope to hand it on to the next generation of students and scholars.

The practices of academic life are not just historical artifacts from a past time (as pragmatism would have it), nor are they simply ways to give people whatever they want (as utilitarians would have it). They are the essential attributes of an academic institution. To lose the practices may mean to lose the good itself. As the political theorist Joseph Raz argues, "some values exist only if there are (or were) social practices sustaining them."[13] Those values must be worth sustaining, but their sustenance cannot be taken for granted.

The stakes, then, are quite high. They concern whether we want colleges to take their cue from students' preexisting preferences, the varied and myriad demands of the world beyond, or from principles internal to education itself. Many college professors, especially those in the arts and sciences, need to own their assumptions and even celebrate them. They believe in practices and virtues that are associated with a liberal education. The best colleges sustain ways of thinking and doing that are threatened in a society dominated by utilitarian and pragmatic modes of thought.

For everyone involved in discussions of the future of college education, however, being aware that we speak different languages may help us engage with one another more thoughtfully. It will no doubt help us understand why we so often seem to be talking past each other.

Context

CHAPTER ONE

On Disruptive Innovation

EVERYWHERE ONE turns, the idea of disruptive innovation continues to spread. The idea of disruptive innovation posits that old institutions, including colleges and universities, will be hard-pressed to change quickly enough to meet a fast-changing world. Instead, new technologies and organizations will outcompete the old, even if—and, in fact, because—the new ones offer subpar but cheaper products. In time, the new institutions will cultivate demand for their products, improve quality, and displace the older institutions, which did not change fast enough. This happens in Silicon Valley, and it will soon happen to campuses across America.[1]

The rhetoric of disruptive innovation combines a theory of organizational change with a theory of time. Existing institutions find innovation difficult because their structures and norms are oriented around doing, and even improving, what they already do—a phenomenon political scientists call path dependence. Agile new institutions can enter the market because there is demand for more suppliers, and they are not beholden to the past. But such claims have often been married to the presumption that new technologies have sped up the rate of social change, making existing institutions even more vulnerable. And it is this piece—the narrative of speed—that has led so many advocates of disruption to believe that we must act now or be left behind.

The narrative of speed is quickly spreading. For instance, the authors of the Spellings Report, issued in 2006 by a commission appointed by then US Secretary of Education Margaret Spellings, concluded that higher education is a "mature enterprise." "History is littered with examples of industries that, at their peril," did not respond to a changing society, the report warned. New technology and global competition mandate a fundamental transformation of education institutions.[2]

In the wake of the decision by the University of Virginia's Board of Visitors to remove university president Teresa Sullivan in 2012, the board's rector at the time, Helen Dragas, asserted that the institution was facing an "existential threat." The times, Dragas claimed, call for a bolder leader than Sullivan, someone willing to impose "a much faster pace of change in administrative structure, in governance, in financial resource development and in resource prioritization and allocation." "The world," Dragas proclaimed, "is simply moving too fast."[3]

Old-Fashioned Reforms

Policy makers and university administrators who advocate disruptive innovation are right that all institutions—and colleges and universities are no exception—must account for changing external environments. No institution is ever static, but proclamations to adapt or die ignore the fact that human environments are the products of human agency. Society is a human construct, not a natural process. Institutions can shape as well as reflect the society and culture around them.

Despite all the talk of disruptive innovation, what is perhaps most surprising is how familiar and uninteresting recent models of disruptive innovation really are. Yes, they use computers, but the structures of institutions like Western Governors University, Southern New Hampshire University's College for America, and the ever-expanding Arizona State University online programs are really premised on ideas from the Industrial Revolution.[4] Managers control the organization. Labor is subdivided into discrete tasks and laborers alienated from the products of their work. In turn, those products—including curriculum and assessment—are standardized and work is routinized. This model is quite old-fashioned.[5]

By contrast, forward-looking companies try to emulate traditional colleges by building large, idyllic campuses, where people can interact and be creative.[6] "There is something magical about sharing meals," said former Google CFO Patrick Pichette on why Google discourages telecommuting. "There is something magical about spending the time together, about noodling on ideas, about asking at the computer, 'What do you think of this?'" That sounds a lot like the traditional college experience, but, in new-model universities, fundamental aspects of traditional ones—such as personalized teaching, green lawns, academic freedom, shared governance, meaningful exposure to the liberal arts and sciences, and time and autonomy for reflection—are deemed irrelevant.[7]

Take the argument that Michael Crow, president of Arizona State University, made in his coauthored 2015 book, *Designing the New American University*. Because expanding access to college degrees requires innovation, and because it wanted to move fast, ASU embraced technology to outsource teaching through, in Crow's words, "partnerships to expand and improve the online learning experience, utilizing over one hundred third-party tools and services." Instructional designers worked with faculty to design online courses that faculty members once taught. "Coaches," teaching assistants, and adjuncts teach online to students who might have had access to professors on campuses.[8]

Paul LeBlanc, president of Southern New Hampshire University, celebrates the same reforms at his institution's online College for America. In a 2013 statement to the US Senate Committee on Health, Education, Labor, and Pensions, LeBlanc told senators that "not having traditional instructional faculty is not proving to be a problem. We use academics to construct the learning and to do the assessments, but not in any traditional instructional role. Students, working with the aid of a dedicated SNHU coach (or adviser), access rich learning content, their own resources and each other, and it is proving very effective thus far."[9]

What makes such reforms so hard to resist is the presumption that the world is moving too fast to take stock. All hands must be on deck. The ship is sinking. Legislators are impatient. Faculty members are complacent. But is this true? Is the world changing so fast that all the things colleges and universities are supposed to do and have done have been rendered irrelevant? Are the forces of disruption really that powerful?

The Value of Continuity

To even start answering these questions, we must examine the assumption that all of society is changing too fast for reflection. How do we know that today is moving faster than yesterday? Are we not just importing a storyline that might be true for one sphere of our lives—technology— into other spheres, where change is slower? Does a story that emanates from Silicon Valley belong or even explain change elsewhere? Is all human activity subject to the same accelerating forces as technological innovation? Can we speed everything up? Should we?

In a 2008 essay, sociologist Hartmut Rosa raises the concern that our world is experiencing desynchronized rates of change. He argues that while technological change may be happening very fast, other realms of our shared lives cannot be equally sped up. That includes, he notes, democratic politics. Bold leaders who believe that the world is changing too fast have little patience for "the political system's fundamental inability to accelerate." But "democratic political decision making" is always slow, Rosa writes, because "processes of deliberation and aggregation in a pluralistic democratic society inevitably take time."[10]

The same is true for higher education. Some parts of our world may be changing fast, but it's not clear that one can speed up the rate of change in higher education without significant damage. Yet the narrative of speed, imported from the world of technology into the world of education, serves powerful interests. When we believe we have no time to slow down because the world is changing too fast, we prevent ourselves from asking what kinds of institutions we need. We raise our hands in surrender to what appear to be inexorable forces but are just human aspirations. To those who believe that all spheres of society are changing as fast as technology, there is no time to wait for those not already on board. The only way to stay afloat is to allow visionaries at the top to act boldly. Other people should follow along or be left behind.

Innovators dismiss those who might want to slow down and think, or who worry about what might be lost. We must not sit around and watch faculty members "deliberate while shifts in policy, culture and technology flash by at warp speed," ASU's Crow proclaims.[11] There is no time for shared governance.

What these visionaries ignore is that institutions and ideas do not become outdated just as Apple computers do. While the radicalism of disruption may capture our imaginations, scholars have noted that the theory does not always explain what actually happens.[12] In some ways, disruptive innovation is a language of change, but it is not always a description of the reality of change. As Harvard University historian Jill Lepore has written, disruptive innovation is "not a law of nature. It's an artifact of history, an idea, forged in time; it's the manufacture of a moment of upsetting and edgy uncertainty. Transfixed by change, it's blind to continuity."[13]

But we need continuity, too. Indeed, higher education's capacity to evolve slowly may be one of its chief virtues. Yes, today's colleges and universities are vastly different from those of centuries past. As disruptive innovators condescendingly remind us, however, much remains the same. Colleges continue to have campuses with leafy quads and professors and classrooms. At graduation, collegians still wear caps and gowns. It is this ability of colleges to design spaces insulated from fast change that enables them to maintain forms of knowing that might otherwise disappear, to invest in scholarship that takes decades to pay off, and to educate students with ideas and perspectives that are not always prevalent in public discourse.

The real problem we face is that colleges and universities today are changing too quickly, not too slowly. Tradition has not been strong enough to withstand external pressure. In such a context, true courage requires saying that enough is enough. It requires defending the college or university as an academic institution. It requires making clear that some things are worth saving and even savoring—that continuity has benefits. It requires attributing long-term trends, such as the erosion of tenure or the decline of the liberal arts and public funding, to human beings rather than to disruptive technologies. We should celebrate the fact that academic life moves slowly. Research takes time. Teaching does, too. To educate a human being requires her or him to step outside of the busyness of daily life. Developing new skills and knowledge takes years. It is even harder to inculcate in students such intellectual virtues as curiosity. It harms colleges' and universities' research and teaching mission to give in to the narrative of speed (see chapter 7).[14]

If we had courage, we would acknowledge that education cannot be done by machines or be done too fast. We would argue that true learning depends on the cultivation of personal relationships.[15] We would conclude, based on the evidence, that the best way to improve student success is to put students on campuses that set high expectations and emphasize the liberal arts and sciences.[16] Maybe we would invoke the work of cognitive scientists or biologists who have explored why real learning is tough and takes trust and time.[17] Perhaps we would even stand up for the humanistic and civic goals of liberal education.

In short, we would argue that all students deserve access to real campuses and professors. We would urge legislators to help all students, of any age or background, afford the time it takes to get a college education. We would note that this is particularly true for disadvantaged and first-generation college students, who do not benefit from the kinds of reforms disruptors advocate, at least if we want to offer access to a meaningful education and not just to degrees.

Instead of making the case for what works, the disruptors have lost faith that colleges and universities can resist external forces of change. They thus seek to tear down the walls between the institution and the world, forgetting that those walls are not just problems but also solutions. By creating spaces for intellectual refuge and reflection, colleges and universities provide something rare and necessary for our society. Disruptors often portray themselves as heroic agents of change. In reality, they are giving in by giving up. To run from forces that seem too large to counter is human, but this response should not be mistaken for fortitude or moral courage.

These are hard times, no doubt, for higher education. Colleges and universities face many pressures. It will take a lot of strength to meet new needs and new environments without sacrificing the academy's core principles and practices. It will take some resistance, too. We must be sympathetic with administrators who are fearful of the future and feel powerless to change it. They, more than faculty members, must respond to legislators' and their own boards' demands to offer more degrees cheaper and faster. Nonetheless, those of us who—as citizens, legislators, administrators, faculty members, and students— want to pass down the opportunities we have had to future students and professors, and who aspire to increase access to it for first-generation students, must have the courage of our convictions. We must remember what colleges and universities are for and ensure that those purposes are sustained, even as our institutions continue to evolve. In short, we must respond deliberatively, not out of fear that the world is moving too fast for thought.

CHAPTER TWO

On Two Recent Occasions

From maine to California, policy makers are pressing America's colleges to offer cheaper and faster degrees. They want colleges to focus on job training. Leaders from both parties complain about the failure of colleges to prepare young people for the workforce, and they portray college leaders and professors as behind the times. They want change, and they want it now.

There is an almost endless list of recent events that exemplify these efforts, and there are stories from almost every state in the Union. The two occasions below have been chosen because they illuminate clearly the principles behind many reforms today. The first occasion is the University of North Carolina's Board of Governors' decision to appoint Margaret Spellings, President George W. Bush's Secretary of Education, to lead its campuses in 2015. The second concerns a 2016 controversy over the embrace, by Simon Newman, president of Maryland's Mount St. Mary's University, of both business practices and job training at the expense of undergraduate liberal education.

Spellings and Newman are not alone. Instead, they were chosen because their ideas are representative of the dominant voices in higher education reform today. They both believe that colleges and universities must become more responsive to students' and employers' preferences and the changing economy. They endorse utilitarian and pragmatic approaches to the challenges facing American higher education.

Occasion 1: North Carolina, 2015

In 2015, Margaret Spellings was chosen by the University of North Carolina's Board of Governors to lead the state's sixteen-campus system.[1] In selecting Spellings, the UNC Board of Governors chose one of higher education's leading visionaries and critics. As US Secretary of Education, Spellings had put together one of the highest-profile commissions on higher education in American history. In 2006, the commission issued the Spellings Report, or as it is formally known, *A Test of Leadership: Charting the Future of U.S. Higher Education*.[2] In this report, we see

Spellings's aspiration for the future of American higher education.

The Spellings Report proposed to transform the purpose and structure of American higher education to ensure "future economic growth." Students need credentials and skills to get ahead, and employers want programs and research that meet their needs. Thus, the report sought a higher education system "that creates new knowledge, contributes to economic prosperity and global competitiveness, and empowers citizens." When one reads the whole report, however, it becomes clear that only the central phrase mattered to the authors. There is nothing in the report that recognizes the need for basic noncommercial research in the arts and sciences, or that states why intellectual inquiry is good on its own terms. Citizenship barely registers in the rest of the document. The commission's report completely ignores the American tradition of liberal general education. In fact, the phrases "liberal education" and "liberal arts" do not even appear in the document. Citizens, then, need to be empowered to get ahead, but not to be part of a democratic polity.

While the report seeks to promote "social mobility," it does not seek to expand students' access to the knowledge offered by a college education; it wants to develop what the report calls "intellectual capital." This is made clear by what the report states to be the "value of higher education"—to feed the "new knowledge-driven economy."

In fact, the civic and other benefits of a college education are presented as by-products and not as purposes of going to college. In the section "Findings regarding the Value of Higher Education," at the end of a long list concerning "the transformation of the world economy" and the relationship between degrees and salaries, the report acknowledges as an afterthought that college education "produces broader social gains." Yet the report clearly places the civic and cultural purposes of college education as secondary to the economic: "Colleges and universities are major economic engines, while also serving as civic and cultural centers."

In the section titled "Findings regarding Learning," the meaning of citizenship is linked to people "who are able to lead and compete in the 21st-century global marketplace," not people who care and think deeply about the public welfare because they have received a serious general education in the arts and sciences. According to the report, the purpose of learning is not to gain wisdom, ethics, or insight but to develop intellectual capital or, stated more clearly, to reduce one's mind to a profit-generating entity that improves one's own salary while serving the needs of American business.

The Spellings Report recognizes that higher education exists in a "consumer-driven environment," but rather than resist the commodification of education, it instead uses this as context to argue that student-consumers care little about "whether a college has for-profit or nonprofit status" and whether classes are online or in buildings. The report ignores the simple fact that students are not consumers but students, and therefore institutions of learning have the responsibility to educate those who do not yet know what they are seeking or what they need. To treat education as just another market good responding to consumer demand is to mistake its very nature.

Because the commissioners expected resistance from traditional higher education institutions, the report embraced all the buzzwords that have come to be associated with the idea of disruptive innovation. Its authors presume that higher education is a "mature enterprise." "History is littered with examples of industries that, at their peril," did not respond to a changing society, the report warns. New technology and global competition mandate a fundamental transformation of educational institutions. Given the growing cost of tuition, and given that "the prospects for a return to a time of generous state subsidies are not good," the report urges "a focused program of cost cutting and productivity improvements."

The question, then, is how these cuts and productivity gains will be achieved. While the report does not explicitly advocate doing away with expensive things like faculty members with tenure and academic freedom, and campuses with classrooms in which students interact with professors, these goals are hinted at. The report explicitly embraces "new providers and new paradigms, from for-profit universities to distance learning." It urges states to promote "both traditional and electronic delivery of college courses in high school."

The report aspires to see "the dissemination of technological advances in teaching that lower costs on a quality-adjusted basis." It urges the elimination of "regulatory and accreditation barriers to new models in higher education that will increase supply and drive costs down." That final phrase refers to institutions like Western Governors University, which, as I have argued elsewhere, eliminates the traditional role of faculty members, offers no meaningful liberal education, and outsources curricular design. (Western Governors' then president, Robert Mendenhall, was one of the report's commissioners.)[3]

Finally, the report embraces the accountability movement. It advocates a national "consumer-friendly" database, a recommendation that President Obama made one of his priorities. His College Scorecard offered the public information about institutions' cost, graduation rates, and graduates' salaries, reinforcing the Spellings Report's presumption that a successful college generates intellectual capital as measured by graduates' earnings.

The Spellings Commission's ideas and conclusions did not, of course, emerge from terra nova. For decades, the "culture wars" have convinced conservative critics that liberal professors in the arts and sciences are not to be trusted. But if the professors can't be trusted, policy makers have had to find a group of people they could trust. They found those people in the business community. Yet business leaders are no less biased than college professors.

While many in the business world no doubt value their own liberal education, when it comes to higher education, at least according to the Spellings Report, employers want graduates who meet the workforce's needs. They want skills, but there is nothing in the report to suggest that the report's authors (or its sponsors, like Spellings) or employers care about the actual knowledge and insights that come from a good college education.

The shift to treating college education as a consumer good also reflects a broader decline in our faith in the authority of colleges and universities. Faculty members themselves lost faith that they have something to teach young people. Over time, core curricula gave way to electives, as exemplified by Brown University's 1969 New Curriculum, which removed all general requirements in order to empower students to find their own way to the truth.[4] Brown's approach at least was intellectual, but across America, colleges and universities sought to appeal to consumer tastes. They offered the programs that students wanted along with the pools, climbing walls, and other amenities that they desired. It is not surprising that business is today the largest undergraduate major in America.

Finally, the UNC case demonstrates a changing understanding of the role of trustees. Groups such as the American Council of Trustees and Alumni have prodded university trustees to play a more active managerial role in shaping their institutions. They urge trustees to defer less to presidents and faculty. Yet, as the former University of Virginia president John T. Casteen III wrote in the wake of the UVa Board of Visitors' own efforts at disruptive innovation, "trustees are fiduciaries—legally responsible for assets, financial and other. As a condition of office, they accept obligations to sustain assets that do not belong to them, and to serve the interests of others." They are "people with obligations, not people with powers," and the heart of their obligation is to ensure that the institutions with which they are entrusted carry out their purpose.[5]

What is that purpose? What is the end of a college or university? Trusteeship entails responsibility for that purpose, not efforts at disrupting it. According to Margaret Spellings, colleges and universities do not exist to cultivate the life of the mind. Intellectual exploration does not count if it cannot be commercialized or be proven to generate "intellectual capital." In reality, Spellings's report offers a vision of the university without its academic purposes, personnel, or practices. In short, Spellings forces us to ask whether American colleges and universities ought to be academic institutions. By hiring her, the members of UNC's Board of Governors made their answer to that question known.

Occasion 2: Maryland, 2016

The expanding controversy over President Simon Newman's words and actions at Mount St. Mary's University, a Catholic college in Maryland, provided an opportunity to reflect on how much has changed since a previous Newman, Cardinal John Henry Newman, wrote his still widely read *The Idea of a University* in 1853. Cardinal Newman was writing at a time when the German ideal of research was transforming universities on both sides of the

Atlantic Ocean. Simon Newman became president of his university at a time when higher education institutions are being asked to redefine themselves to produce employable graduates.

John Henry Newman, a convert to Catholicism, was ordained in Rome in 1846. In November 1851, he was called to serve as rector of the newly established Catholic University of Ireland, a post he held for seven years. With his discourses, published in 1853, he sought to lay out the mission of a Catholic university for both lay and Catholic audiences.

Cardinal Newman's *The Idea of a University* opens with a simple statement: a university "is a place of *teaching* universal *knowledge*. That implies that its object is, on the one hand, intellectual, not moral; and on the other, that it is the diffusion and extension of knowledge rather than the advancement." To Newman, if the university's "object were scientific and philosophical discovery, I do not see why a university should have students; if religious training, I do not see how it can be the seat of literature and science." Cardinal Newman was not rejecting the Church's role but focusing attention on the specific intellectual purpose of university studies. He believed that the Church "steadies" the university "in the performance of that office." He also ultimately did not reject the principle of university research, but sought to temper it.[6]

Cardinal Newman believed that a university must emphasize students' intellectual development: "to discover and to teach are distinct functions." A university must place the students' "spiritual welfare" at the center of its activities. It must focus its energies on "the culture of the intellect." It must teach each student to seek truth.

He also focused his attention on why a university must be a place for liberal education. Liberal education introduced a student to "an intellectual tradition" that endowed him with "the great outlines of knowledge, the principles on which it rests, the scale of its parts, its lights and its shades, its great points and its little, as he otherwise cannot apprehend them." But to what end? Here, Newman insisted, "knowledge is capable of being its own end." Liberal education, compared to professional education, "stands on its own pretensions" and "refuses to be *informed* (as it is called) by any end, or absorbed into any art, in order to duly present itself to our contemplation."[7]

Cardinal Newman was resisting various tendencies of his time. He was defending the premise that a Catholic university should emphasize the liberal arts and sciences. He was arguing that teaching was a practice sufficiently distinct from specialized research to require its own institutions, and he was articulating an idea of liberal education that was not focused on practicality or professional education. A university, and especially a Catholic university, stood for particular goods. If those goods did not guide the institution, then it should not be called a university.

Simon Newman comes from a very different background. After earning bachelor's and master's degrees in the sciences from the University of Cambridge, he went to Stanford University to receive his MBA. Having had thirty years in the business and finance worlds and having served as director of JP Capital Partners and as CEO of Cornerstone Management Group, he aspired to do with the university what any entrepreneur seeks to do with her or his start-up: "raise a lot of capital and start a lot of programs and start the university on a more aggressive growth trajectory."[8] Perhaps he did not realize that a university is not a firm—that its purposes are complex and human and cannot be boiled down to data sets.

That at least seems to be the case in the controversy over dismissing struggling students—which he infamously described as a need to "drown the bunnies."[9] On the one hand, as Newman noted in an essay in the *Washington Post*, it makes sense to identify struggling students early so as to protect them and their families from unjustifiable debt burdens. On the other hand, Newman reportedly was also seeking to raise his institution's retention rate by removing students before the date when the university must report its numbers to the federal government.[10]

The focus on outcomes reflects a broader transformation in how we think about successful institutions. Whereas once business schools portrayed firms as complex institutions responsible to multiple stakeholders, they now emphasize managers' responsibility to overcome what is called the principal-agent problem in order to maximize shareholder value. Owners, as principals, have clear interests, but employees, as agents, do not always share them. To align agents to serve the will of owners, managers must impose clear performance measures and accountability.[11] That approach is more challenging in the nonprofit and public sectors, where maximizing profit is not necessarily the best way to evaluate institutional success. But the basic approach—setting external standards and imposing incentives and penalties to hold institutions accountable—was adopted in what is known as the New Public Management, which is one of the principles animating President Obama's College Scorecard.[12]

Simon Newman's business background made him comfortable in this new regulatory environment. He sought to maximize value, but the issue is about defining value. What counts? Should a desire to report higher retention rates trump the institution's responsibility to the students it enrolls? More important, if one accepts the notion of principal-agent theory, one also imagines the university as a firm with managers and employees and sees the role of managers as aligning all employees to meeting the firm's stated outcomes. That makes shared governance a real problem.

Cardinal Newman had argued that a university is at the end of the day a community of "teachers and learners" gathered together, as John Schwenkler writes. But, Schwenkler, an assistant professor of philosophy at Florida State University who previously taught at Mount St. Mary's, continues, if "the faculty of a university are the university," then "the institutional structure of the modern university, and its oversight by administrators, politicians and boards of trustees, are inessential to what it is."

This is because the "fundamental core" of what constitutes a university is, and has long been, "the guild of scholars dedicated to the activity of universal learning."[13] Universities, from this perspective, are not firms with owners and employees, but that was not how Simon Newman saw it when he demoted the provost and summarily fired two faculty members, one with tenure, who questioned his policies.

Simon Newman's idea of a university is fundamentally different from Cardinal Newman's. Rather than emphasize the university's Catholic traditions and commitment to liberal arts education, the president allegedly asked why there were so many crucifixes on the campus. While that might just be a matter of taste, he also purportedly complained that "liberal arts doesn't sell."[14] He expressed his desire to reduce the number of core courses and increase the number of degrees with market value.

Mount St. Mary's website offered no indication that the university was committed to the intellectual culture of its students. The lead page (as of February 15, 2016) extolled Mount St. Mary's not as a place for the mind but as one "in the middle of everything."[15] The university was not a place apart, but a gateway to internships in DC and rock climbing and paddle boarding. When one clicked on the button "Learn Here," the first thing one saw was "BizHack, where students and professionals collaborate to create entrepreneurial business plans for products and services for the future."[16] This is an institution that appears to be oriented not to students' minds but to their pocketbooks. It's not even clear that it has a liberal arts mission. Indeed, when one clicked on the button "Succeed Anywhere," the university did not talk about students becoming better people or citizens but about their getting better jobs at leading firms.[17]

In a letter that Mr. Newman emailed to parents in response to the growing controversy over his comments about drowning bunnies and his dismissal of faculty members, he sought to reassure the Mount St. Mary's community that he was on the side of progress. The university is "in growth mode, and on the move. We are transforming our 200-year-old Catholic university to meet the needs of a demanding global economy. Your student is a part of this exciting transformation. We are building on our existing liberal arts core and Catholic intellectual tradition and preparing students for a more technical skills-based job market in a way that only the Mount can."[18]

Thus, in the tale of two Newmans, we can see many of the questions that remain at the heart of much broader conversations about college education. What is the role of faith in college education? What is the relationship between teaching and research? What ought to constitute college education? Should colleges focus on the intellectual development of their students or cater to students' economic aspirations and the needs of employers? Does something set a college apart from other institutions?

Both Newmans grappled with how to define the essence of college education during historical moments when colleges were—and are—under pressure to modernize to meet the needs of a changing society and to justify what they do. They both thus offer us a chance to reflect on where we have been, where we are, and where we might want to go next.

CHAPTER THREE

On For-Profit Schools

CRITICS OF efforts to regulate for-profit colleges proclaimed that advocates of regulation during the Obama administration were waging a "war" on for-profit universities. Under the Trump administration, Secretary of Education Betsy DeVos promised to ease back on these regulations. She appointed a former dean of the for-profit DeVry University to be the Education Department's for-profit fraud investigator. She made clear that she considers, at the K–12 and higher education levels, for-profits to be one of the solutions to America's education problems.[1]

The reality is exactly the opposite: the for-profit sector is challenging a centuries-old practice of separating philanthropy from business. Since the Elizabethan statute of charitable uses in 1601, Anglo-American law has sought to encourage charitable giving to promote the common good. The idea behind modern philanthropy is that nonprofits undertake services that are either inappropriate for market activity or would not be supported by the market. To ensure that these goods are available, the state provides them itself through public institutions, and also offers private nonprofits legal privileges (such as incorporation), economic incentives (such as tax benefits), and direct financial support.

In 1874, Massachusetts passed one of the earliest general laws exempting from taxation any "educational, charitable, benevolent, or religious" institution. Believing that citizens, not just the state, should promote the common good, Massachusetts sought to encourage citizens to devote their money to institutions that would serve the public. Implicit was the assumption that certain kinds of activities—educational, charitable, benevolent, and religious—should be done as a service and not for a profit. Massachusetts's law became a model for other states.

In the modern era, tax incentives are one of the primary ways in which the state supports nonprofit institutions, whether they be churches, local grassroots associations, or colleges and universities. The state also subsidizes nonprofits that serve the community, especially in social services and education. Americans have not only given generously but also benefited greatly from philanthropy.[2]

This is not to suggest that the history of American

philanthropy is without conflict. After the American
Revolution, many Americans worried about what Anglo-
Americans called the "dead hand of the past." Thomas
Jefferson was among them. He believed that permanent
endowments enabled one generation to influence the
affairs of the next in ways that threatened democracy.
"The earth belongs in usufruct to the living; . . . [and] the
dead have neither powers nor rights over it," proclaimed
Jefferson in 1789.

These questions reemerged in the twentieth century. Many Americans reacted with great concern when
Andrew Carnegie and others used their wealth to engage
in philanthropic endeavors that some opposed. During
the Cold War, foundation-sponsored research led some
policy makers to question foundations' power and political agenda. Similar concerns can be raised about the Gates
Foundation today. Their wealth may give private philan-
thropies undue influence in public deliberation. Philanthropy, no less than business, requires regulation.[3]

Moreover, public and nonprofit institutions become
corrupted when profit becomes their goal rather than a
means of fulfilling their mission. This has happened to
some extent in American universities that invest in tan-
gentially related programs, such as big-time sports. Since
the passage of the Bayh-Dole Act (1980), which permits
universities to profit from publicly funded research, colleges and universities have encouraged marketable rather
than socially beneficial science. Moreover, in an era of
state defunding, many policy makers are urging colleges

and universities to act more like businesses, even when doing so perverts their mission and institutional culture.[4]

The state must ensure that both public and nonprofit institutions remain true to their civic mission in return for the legal and financial benefits they receive. This point was made by Robert Zemsky, a member of the Spellings Commission during the George W. Bush administration. Zemsky urged colleges to talk constantly "about purposes, about ends rather than means," to hold fast against the temptations of profit.[5] But for-profit institutions consistently fail this test; the evidence shows that for-profit institutions spend less money on instruction, devote their resources to marketing, and leave students deep in debt in order to make a profit. That, at least, is what the US Senate's Committee on Health, Education, Labor, and Pensions concluded.[6] Indeed, for-profits have notoriously targeted America's most vulnerable, people who are struggling to make ends meet. Rather than serve them, however, too many for-profits have taken advantage of them, offering higher-cost and lower-quality degrees to Americans who deserve better.[7]

Whether colleges are for-profit or not matters a lot. It affects their mission, their culture, their labor practices, and the lessons that they offer students. As Michael Sandel notes, "markets change the character of the goods and social practices they govern."[8] For-profit education implies that education is a commodity bought for the advantage it provides. It makes no pretense that *service* is a necessary part of being a college graduate. In fact, even if it did, students are too smart to believe it. They know what they are buying—a degree from a vendor. We expect businesses to make money, but we want our churches and schools to treat us as congregants and students, not as consumers.

This is not just semantics. Economists also recognize that education and other services, including medicine, are not like other market goods. First, they are public goods in that their benefits are not exclusive to the recipient. Second, they depend on expertise. Unlike the purchaser of a television set, students, like patients, depend on the provider since they lack the knowledge to judge quality effectively. This requires trust and depends on limiting the potential for profiteering. Finally, because education is labor intensive, for them to make money, for-profits have incentives to cut costs in ways that also cut quality.[9]

For-profits must be regulated as businesses. They are not charities, despite being subsidized heavily by public student loan dollars.[10] In reality, in return for these public subsidies, for-profits should live by the same rules as nonprofits. They should make the common good their primary goal and reinvest all revenue to fulfill their mission. They will not, however, because they exist to generate wealth for investors and shareholders. As recent scandals have made clear, for-profit institutions in higher education, like other Wall Street businesses, too often put their bottom line ahead of the common good.[11]

For-profit higher education's advocates are declaring war on American philanthropy. They seek to profit off of charity, transforming what should be a service into another way to gain wealth. They threaten a distinction that has deep roots in American history and law. They suggest that all goods—including education, charity, and religion—should be commodities. History and recent evidence tell us otherwise. While the line between the for-profit and nonprofit sectors can be blurry at times, the differences between them are very real, of moral significance, and worthy of protection.

Curriculum

CHAPTER FOUR

On STEM

A WIDELY READ piece in the *New York Times*, titled "A Rising Call to Promote STEM Education and Cut Liberal Arts Funding" (Feb. 21, 2016), told the now well-known story of American policy leaders offering incentives to major in the STEM fields (science, technology, engineering, math), while cutting funding or offering disincentives to major in the humanities and social sciences. One round in this ongoing conversation was spurred by Kentucky governor Matt Bevin's suggestion that tax dollars should fund "useful" degrees, not French literature.[1] Ironically, despite these calls to arms, the United States may actually be producing too many

STEM graduates relative to the economy's actual needs. Far from a shortage of STEM workers, we may have a surplus of engineers and computer scientists.[2]

Lost in this discussion, however, are the ways in which the language of STEM has transformed the orientation, practices, and meaning of science and math. In theory, there are two major faculties on American college campuses: those who teach in the liberal arts and sciences, and those who offer professional education in such fields as business, education, engineering, social work, and various health and technology programs. The two types of faculties are not necessarily in opposition, but they have different missions because they are oriented toward different goals. In other words, they seek distinct goods.

To faculty in the arts and sciences, undergraduate education is liberal in nature—it is about gaining a broad knowledge of how the human and natural worlds work, because doing so can inspire students and because the public good is well served by well-educated citizens and leaders. Ideally, and often, there is no specific vocational outcome to these majors. In fact, to ask a history, English, biology, or geology major, "What are you going to do with that?" ought to be irrelevant since these are academic disciplines designed for academic purposes. When majors were first established, their goal was not job training but intellectual depth or, better put, enhancing a general education. Thus, majors in the arts and sciences exist for their educational purposes with no real or necessary relation to market needs.

Professional faculty, on the other hand, train people for specific jobs. Their success is measured by whether their students gain the knowledge and skills necessary for employment in specific fields. Students who major in engineering, for example, are right to ask their programs, "What can I do with that?" Moreover, students who choose to major in these fields may not receive the same kind of liberal education as those in the arts and sciences. Instead, they seek a direct line to employment. These fields, in other words, are tied closely to market needs.

The rhetoric of STEM professionalizes science faculty by reorienting their core community of identity to be with vocational engineering and technology professors instead of their colleagues in the liberal arts and sciences. But the sciences are not job training; they are part of liberal education. Math too is a liberal pursuit.[3] Ideally, faculty and students in the sciences and math have different goals, perspectives, and aspirations than do those in engineering and technology-related fields. Thus, traditionally, science and math faculty have identified themselves with the broader purposes of liberal education, of which they are a part.

The more we use the term STEM—in praise, condemnation, or simply as a descriptor—the more we risk dividing the arts and sciences faculty from each other. The arts and sciences exist as the educational core of the undergraduate collegiate curriculum. They are tied together conceptually. There is no difference, from the perspective of liberal education, between majoring in philosophy or chemistry. Professors in both disciplines, in all the arts and sciences, believe in the value of intellectual pursuit, in fostering curiosity about the world, and in graduating students who have breadth and depth. Yet, increasingly on campuses across the United States, colleges of arts and sciences are dividing into two units, the humanities and social sciences in one, and the sciences and math in another. This is not simply a bureaucratic question. The organization of colleges and universities reflects how we conceptualize knowledge.

To the extent that faculty in the sciences and math see themselves as sharing a similar mission to that of engineering and technology represents a significant change in what it means to be a scientist or mathematician, STEM transforms scientists and mathematicians into professional rather than liberal educators. It weakens the idea of liberal education as something that requires and encompasses the humanities and the social and natural sciences, making it easier for commentators to pit the sciences and math against the "liberal arts," and it encourages scientists to think of themselves in these terms rather than as part of a larger community of scholars engaged in the pursuit and transmission of knowledge.[4]

The natural sciences were not always essential to liberal education. For the first half of the nineteenth century, science was seen as too practical, too worldly to be part of a liberal education. Certainly, some basic courses in "natural philosophy" were part of the collegiate curriculum, but the core remained ancient languages and literature, history, political economy, and ethics. By the late nine-teenth century, however, the claim that natural science was not a legitimate academic pursuit and that science should not be taught at colleges was no longer tenable.

In fact, by the early twentieth century, science had become a key component of liberal education. Not only did humanistic disciplines embrace the "scientific" research model, but scientists argued that the scien-tific approach to knowledge—experimental, constantly changing, innovative—was the best way to train demo-cratic citizens. Democracies needed citizens who could ask questions, test hypotheses, reach deliberate judg-ments, and then change those judgments if they proved faulty. Science taught these essential critical thinking skills and virtues.[5] In other words, science joined the lib-eral arts because scientists and others believed that the sci-ences offered a vital contribution to liberal education in a democracy.

In more recent decades, we have seen the slow erosion of science as part of liberal education. If the liberal arts and sciences are noncommercial, we have witnessed the increasing commercialization of scientific research, espe-cially after the Bayh-Dole Act (1980) encouraged colleges and universities and their science faculty to monetize their research. In response to declining public funding, university-based scientific research is increasingly about developing products with market value. Basic research for the public good—or, the research side of the liberal arts and sciences mission—is becoming less important.

Before 1981, American academic scientists produced fewer than two hundred fifty patents per year. That number has grown steadily. In 2003, American universities filed around eight thousand patents. Between 1980 and 2000, American universities also established 3,376 start-up companies based on the work of university scientists. While most research does not rely on industry funding, industry funding is the fastest growing segment of funding for university science. As one scholar concludes, "higher education is in an unprecedented period of interface between the academy and industry."[6]

This transforms how we imagine the ideal college graduate. If the liberal arts and sciences aspire to develop human beings and citizens, the sciences and math are now seen by policy makers and the public as primarily about developing skilled workers. Thus, in the George W. Bush administration's Spellings Report on higher education's future (see chapter 2), colleges exist to generate "intellectual capital" for a "new knowledge-driven economy." The liberal arts are not even mentioned, and science and technology fields are valued for their impact on the economy. College graduates must be profit centers, not insightful human beings and citizens.[7]

STEM therefore is a term that should be used with caution, if not abandoned altogether. Certainly, we should continue to educate engineers and computer scientists. There is also no doubt that we need students who are better prepared in the natural sciences, for the same reason that we need students to study literature and history. In today's world, it is vital that undergraduates have knowledge of science and math to be effective citizens. And, as with all majors in the arts and sciences, it is also valuable for students to pursue their own intellectual interests in depth to get a sense of what it means to really understand something and to develop higher-order knowledge, skills, and intellectual virtues. Through their majors, students are able to see the world with new eyes.

The STEM rubric undermines the unity between the humanities and the natural sciences. For many policy makers, this is no doubt desirable. Yet, if faculty in the sciences and mathematics are not careful about how they identify themselves, they will be party to the erosion of the ideal of liberal learning, of which they remain an essential part. If faculty in the humanities and social sciences are not careful, they will find themselves marginalized as the sciences abandon liberal education to join forces with market-driven technology and engineering programs. If Americans are not careful, we will soon find that we have fundamentally changed the purposes and goals of collegiate education.

CHAPTER FIVE

On the Humanities

IMAGINE YOURSELF an early teacher of what comes to be known as the *studia humanitatis*, not one of the famous influential ones, but one of the humble teachers earning their keep offering preparatory skills, perhaps at the University of Paris or in one of its adjunct colleges, to students seeking admission to the higher faculties of law, medicine, or theology, or just to get on in life. This humanist was not concerned with imparting knowledge but was instead a purveyor of skills (or arts) inherited from the ancient liberal arts of grammar and rhetoric. The Renaissance humanists, as the scholar Paul Kristeller has written, believed that studying the ancients mattered less for the wisdom they imparted than because ancient texts taught students "to write and speak well."[1]

From Humanism to Philosophy

In our idealized vision of Renaissance humanists, we imagine them seeking to re-create the virtues and knowledge of the ancients, and some of the most renowned did. But, as Anthony Grafton and Lisa Jardine remind us in *From Humanism to the Humanities* (1986), many Renaissance teachers who went by the name *humanist* promised students that their humanist arts had practical value to students seeking to enter universities or the bureaucracies of church and state. Indeed, Grafton and Jardine conclude that the primary goal of the *studia humanitatis* was not the formation of "original scholars and philosopher kings." Instead, the promise of practical literary skills "to produce effective writers and active participants in civic life" would prove the foundation of "every flourishing school of the later sixteenth century, Protestant or Catholic."[2]

By the eighteenth century, however, a new ideal was emerging, one defined by the *philosophe* rather than the humanist. Unlike the humanist, the *philosophe* sought knowledge as her or his end because, its advocates promised, knowledge would liberate people from the chains of ignorance.[3] Francis Bacon urged us to rid ourselves of false idols, and Kant answered the question, What is Enlightenment?, with the answer that it is humanity's release from its "self-imposed immaturity" (1784). *Sapere Aude*.

The shift from literary skills to philosophical knowledge took place first in royal scientific academies, in coffeehouses, and in salons in civil society before it hit the universities. Most colleges and universities in England and British North America remained focused on educating the Christian gentleman through a curriculum that included the trivial skills (logic, grammar, and rhetoric) and the rational truths offered by the quadrivium. The arrival of the research university symbolized Enlightenment's victory over the university and philosophy's victory over the traditional liberal arts.[4] The philosopher as truth seeker replaced the grammarian and rhetorician as master of skills. The liberal sciences—organized bodies of inquiry and knowledge—joined the liberal arts.[5]

A similar transformation took place in high schools, which in the nineteenth century were thought of as "democracy's college."[6] Colonial boys intending higher study would have attended grammar schools to master ancient Greek and Latin to meet college admission requirements.[7] After the Revolution, first private academies and then, in the decades before the Civil War, public high schools offered curricula that went beyond the trivial arts to include the liberal sciences, or what we have come to know as the core academic subjects. As public high schools expanded, they offered more and more Americans access to a liberal education grounded in the knowledge of biology, chemistry, history, literature, and mathematics. This knowledge was seen as liberating for individuals, as well as essential for effective citizenship.

As one 1848 writer put it, society was "ennobled by the possession, or by the influence of enlightened minds." The modern public high school, unlike its predecessor the grammar school, was a home for philosophy.[8]

The Emergence of the Humanities

The rise of philosophy transformed what humanists considered their work. Humanists also became purveyors of the liberal sciences, not the liberal arts. They taught knowledge, not elementary skills. As doctors of *philosophy*, modern humanities professors are organized into scientific disciplines such as English and history. The modern humanities came into existence when philosophical or academic questions merged with philological techniques of textual and historical analysis to produce new disciplines.[9] That is how the *technique* of using history to study texts, for example, became the *science* of history today as practiced by the modern academic discipline.[10]

Most humanities scholars today are committed to the progressive development of knowledge in their discipline. They share with Daniel Coit Gilman, the first president of the Johns Hopkins University, America's first research university, the belief that universities exist to acquire, conserve, refine, and distribute knowledge.[11] Knowledge is the end of the modern university, and its acquisition and distribution, through teaching and publication, is the end of the modern professor. Knowledge is always changing, justifying the need for expertise and requiring the kind of training provided in modern graduate schools. Professors must advance knowledge in their own work and remain "up to date" in their classrooms. College students should develop the ability to acquire and to use knowledge to interpret the world around them effectively and insightfully.

Yet the coat did not always fit. Early philologists sought to edit and to master ancient texts, which would serve as models of refinement. This aspiration—that words can improve the self—was reimagined in the nineteenth century, within the context of nation-states, as the humanities' acculturating capacity. The emerging humanities would put students in touch with the living traditions of their nation, thus preparing them for active life.[12]

As Princeton president Woodrow Wilson put it in his 1902 inaugural address, a response to the scientism of such educators as Gilman, universities had two tasks. Their first and primary task was "the production of a great body of informed and thoughtful men" in undergraduate colleges. This depended on their secondary task: "the production of a small body of trained scholars and investigators." Most undergraduates did not intend to become specialized researchers. Instead, a Princeton education should give undergraduates "elasticity of faculty and breadth of vision, so that they shall have a surplus of mind to expend, not upon their profession only . . . but also upon the broader interests which lie about them, in the spheres in which they are to be, not breadwinners merely, but citizens as well, and in their own hearts, where they are to grow to the stature of real nobility."[13]

The modern humanities professor holds together, in an unstable isotope, the ancient liberal art of grammar, the modern ideal of scientific or philosophical investigation, and responsibility for culture. For most practicing humanities professors, these strands coexist relatively harmoniously. Many draw from each liberally to define their purposes in the classroom, within the larger college or university, and before the public and policy makers. Moreover, there is a creative tension at the intersection of these three ideals. As Geoffrey Galt Harpham argues, the modern humanities "remain themselves unresolved, and thereby keep open the promise of a kind of knowledge that cannot be either divorced from nor reduced to information."[14] Nonetheless, while most colleges and universities retain general writing and numeracy requirements and continue to offer courses on communication and public speaking, colleges and universities are not organized by skills but by academic disciplines.

The Cold War and the Humanities

It is possible that the humanities held together in the twentieth century not because of their internal coherence but thanks to the external pressures imposed by the Cold War. The modern humanities, one of the many unstable isotopes of the nuclear age, was given expression in the *Harvard Redbook* and other documents of post–World War II America. To the authors of the influential *Redbook*, the American student needed a general liberal education to prepare her or him for "life as a responsible human being and citizen," because democratic citizens needed to connect their specialized work to its larger social meaning and context. A general education would expose students, first, to various domains of knowledge, but these domains also cultivated specific capabilities. While the natural sciences taught students to "describe, analyze, and explain," the humanities taught them to "appraise, judge, and criticize." A college student—as democratic citizen— also needed *"to think effectively, to communicate thought, to make relevant judgments, to discriminate among values,"* or, in other words, the skills and aptitudes that might have been cultivated through grammar, rhetoric, and logic. The result would be knowledgeable, thinking citizens capable of protecting democracy from communism.[15]

The Cold War university also, of course, prized research. The infusion of federal dollars, especially in the natural sciences, transformed universities' activities. Although the humanities also benefited from the rising tide, they found themselves in what historian Michael Meranze has called a "structurally subordinate" position. Humanities professors benefited society, according to the logic of the *Redbook* and other early Cold War documents, through teaching, not research. The natural sciences, and even the social sciences, provided knowledge that addressed practical problems, knowledge that was vital to national security, public policy making, and—after the passage of the Bayh-Dole Act (1980), which made it easier for universities to profit from their research—commerce, too.[16] Yet what did the humanities add? Humanities professors promised to teach students to think well and to write well and to have the values of democratic citizens. At the same time, they undertook scientific research to advance knowledge in new disciplines.

The Post–Cold War University

Arguments about the democratic value of the humanities were sustainable as long as the enemy the United States faced was political. We needed thoughtful, effective citizens to combat the menace of communism. Civic concerns had real purchase on policy makers because of the existential intellectual and military threat posed by the Soviet Union. With the end of the Cold War, this justifying framework came crashing down.[17] The new enemy was not political, but economic. Globalization has created new threats to American prosperity. The new economy is high tech, demanding not well-rounded citizens, but highly trained specialists. Slowly, the idea of the liberal arts and sciences broke apart. The natural sciences and mathematics were moved out of the realm of liberal education to join with engineering in a new isotope, called "STEM," in order to prepare students for today's high-demand jobs and to encourage research more aligned with market needs. The humanities could no longer benefit from their dalliance with the natural sciences. Scientists have moved on with their lives, but humanities professors have not yet gotten over the breakup.

The post–Cold War university is no longer committed to the ends that sustained the Cold War humanities. The reasons are of course multicausal: globalization transformed public discourse; the emergence of the mass university brought in many students whose aspirations were practical rather than liberal;[18] the culture wars left left-leaning humanities professors without conservative allies; and declining tax support shifted the costs of attendance to students, privatizing that portion of a college education that was supposed to be a public good and forcing students to see their educations as financial investments.[19] Today, a true education in the arts and sciences is marketed as an elite good for students lucky enough to attend prestigious private schools or perhaps get into public colleges' honors programs.[20] Other people, critics of the humanities imply, need practical skills.

We see the same trends at the K–12 level. During the first Bush administration, advocates of national standards worried that poor and minority students were not gaining access to meaningful subject matter "because," in the words of a Bush administration document, "the focus has been on basic skills." Under the more recent Common Core, on the other hand, subject matter is deemed secondary to the skills required for "college and career readiness." The importance of knowledge for personal growth or effective citizenship is relegated to the sidelines.[21]

Humanities professors did not seek this new world order, but as they respond to it, they are turning back to the skills they impart. The liberal *arts* and the liberal *sciences* are coming apart absent the pressures of the Cold War to hold them together. In column after column, academic and business leaders defend the liberal arts for teaching transferable skills such as communication, creativity, and critical thinking. And no doubt they do. But if the knowledge humanities professors impart does not matter, neither do the disciplines they inhabit.

Today's defenders of the humanities promise students, policy makers, and employers the skills employers want but say less about their subjects' contribution to the education of a free person and an effective citizen or the importance of basic research in the humanities. There is nothing wrong, of course, with arguing that a good education prepares one for work. There is ample evidence that studying the humanities does lead to economic success. It is the definition of work that is also at stake. The humanities should, and do, prepare people to be insightful and productive contributors to our economic well-being, and contributing to the economy is part of our responsibility as members of society.[22] The challenge is when we treat generating human capital as the end of education and conflate human capital with human subjectivity, as political theorist Wendy Brown cautions us in *Undoing the Demos* (2015).

Under a human capital regime, Brown writes, "*knowledge, thought, and training* are valued and desired almost exclusively for their contribution to capital enhancement. . . . It is not sought for developing the capacities of citizens, sustaining culture, knowing the world, or envisioning and crafting different ways of life in common." Instead, education's benefits must be measured by its "return on investment." Over time, Brown anticipates, "skills for twenty-first century jobs [will be] provided by an instructional staff itself organized around market metrics," making unnecessary "the patently anachronistic conceits and trappings of university life and content."[23]

We must think hard about the implications of the arguments that we use to defend the humanities today. Skills are not just transferable; they are also devoted to ends. To what ends are colleges developing in students the skills of close textual analysis and writing? Why do we want students to become critical thinkers? Do we connect the ends of these skills to higher purposes, or do we defend them in terms of their return on investment? Does critical thinking require the knowledge offered by the fast fraying disciplines that define(d) the humanities? How can we prevent the liberal arts from becoming the neoliberal arts?

And so we circle back. Imagine if you will, a humanist today, peddling her or his wares on the edges of an American university, in an adjunct capacity, promising that the skills he or she can teach will pay off in the higher faculties of business, law, or medicine, or in the bureaucracies of state and corporation. This humanist promises that studying historical or literary texts matters less for the insights they offer, but because they can help students learn "to write and speak well."

CHAPTER SIX

On Business Majors

T ODAY, BUSINESS has become the largest undergraduate major in the United States, as more students
enter college because they believe that they have to, not
because they want to or even because they find school
interesting.[1] Their decision is not unreasonable, since the
United States has largely foreclosed alternative paths to
the middle class. Moreover, because public defunding has
made higher education more expensive, students have
been forced to think about their education primarily as an
economic investment; colleges, in turn, have responded to
declining revenue by treating students as customers.

Yet, one cannot help but conclude that the growth of business majors has come at a significant cost to colleges and to the students they serve. In an era when calls to reform higher education are rampant, eliminating undergraduate business majors may be one simple reform that could have dramatic benefits to both colleges and students. While this reform would not require the kind of disruption reformers sometimes seek, it would improve student learning outcomes and refocus colleges on their core mission without imposing a cost on students' future earnings. It would be a significant change, since it would mean colleges would abandon their most popular majors in order to serve students and society better.

Presumably, many of the students choosing to major in business and related degrees believe it will lead to higher salaries. Policy makers, too, have started to evaluate majors—and even colleges—by their graduates' salaries. There are good reasons to question whether this is a legitimate metric because, as former Rochester Institute of Technology president Bill Destler put it, measuring colleges by graduates' salaries "falsely equates a quality education with gainful employment upon graduation."[2] Or, as a writer in *Forbes* observed, the devaluation of the humanities relative to vocational and technical programs "presage[s] a dismal, corporatization of education, where 'work' is the only goal for every student and 'productivity' is the only measure of worth."[3]

Nevertheless, people understandingly want to know that a good college education serves them after graduation, especially as they go on to pursue careers. Many policy makers have expressed a strong preference for job training over liberal education. This chapter thus explores the relationship between majoring in business and future career success, while recognizing that the goal of a college education is not and should not be about maximizing students' incomes, although it may well be about preparing young people to pursue meaningful work after graduation.

Salaries

Let's start by looking at salaries. Some states now track their college graduates' earnings. For example, the University of Texas system tracks five-year median wages for its graduates. At UT-Arlington, the five-year median wage for business administration and management majors was $53,715 and for marketing was $52,863, compared to $48,854 for history, $46,813 for English, $71,530 for chemistry, and $53,197 for biology. The gap is greater for graduates of UT-Austin, where the five-year median salary was $106,117 for business/commerce majors and $68,201 for marketing, compared to $50,586 for history, $47,148 for English, $51,607 for philosophy, $56,087 for chemistry, and $53,672 for biology.[4]

Researchers at the Georgetown University Center for Education and the Workforce found that for students without a graduate degree, median income for business majors was $60,000, compared to $59,000 for the physical sciences, $55,000 for the social sciences, $50,000 for biology and the life sciences, and $47,000 for the humanities.[5] The American Academy of Arts & Sciences' Humanities Indicators found that the median income for business majors with a terminal bachelor's degree in 2012 was around $60,000, compared to around $50,000 for the humanities.[6]

Yet other studies complicate the story. The *Chronicle of Higher Education*'s *2014 Almanac* concluded that pre-professional majors initially make more than academic majors, but that by midcareer the gap has largely been erased.[7] The Hamilton Project found almost no difference in median lifetime earnings between chemistry, political science, marketing, and business management and administration majors.[8] An analysis by the American Association of Colleges and Universities (AAC&U) concluded that over one's career, median annual earnings for humanities majors and professional/preprofessional majors are almost exactly the same, whereas majors in the sciences and mathematics tend to make more. At their peak earnings, humanities majors, the study found, make more than professional/preprofessional majors.[9]

Strikingly, most majors cluster around a common range. A Payscale study found midcareer median salaries for business majors at $72,100, compared to $98,600 for economics, $71,000 for history, $64,700 for English, $81,200 for philosophy, and $97,300 for physics. At the 75th percentile, the midcareer median salary for business majors was $102,000, compared to $145,000 for economics, $93,200 for English, $103,000 for history, $127,000 for philosophy, and $132,000 for physics. For highly paid positions, the arts and sciences do as well as business.[10]

In reality, the difference between most majors may be within the margin of error for many studies, and gender may shape future earnings more than college major. As one analyst noted, "the difference between humanities majors and science majors, in median income and unemployment, seems to be no more than the difference between residents of Virginia and North Carolina. If someone told to me not to move to Charlotte because no one there can make a living, I would never take them seriously. But worried relatives express the same concerns about classics majors every day, with no sounder evidence."[11]

The data is not only contradictory, but also messy. It's not clear, for example, whether majoring in business leads to higher salaries, or whether other factors are more important. For example, because business programs are better integrated with the business community, they offer their students greater access to internships and employers. The most important complicating factor, however, is self-selection. All undergraduates at UT-Austin, for example, may be academically capable, but those who choose to major in business probably see their education primarily as a way to get ahead. Their own desires and aspirations may matter more than their major.

The same, it should be added, may be true of students majoring in the arts and sciences. They may choose non-vocational majors because they are interested in doing work that produces social value or greater personal satisfaction even if it does not maximize their income. Thus, despite earning more, less than 40 percent of business majors report that they had enough money to "do everything I want to do," compared to 45 percent of graduates in the natural sciences and 42 percent of graduates in the humanities. In other words, business majors, even when they make more money, want more money. Moreover, when asked about how satisfied they are with their work, humanities majors were in every measure (opportunities to advance, salary, benefits, job security, and job location) within five percentage points of degree holders in other fields.[12]

Benefits of Liberal Education

The evidence suggests that there is no reason to conclude that majoring in the liberal arts and sciences will have a negative impact on students' earning potential. Indeed, majoring in the arts and sciences may actually improve graduates' prospects.[13] According to an AAC&U study, employers overwhelmingly desire college students to get a liberal education, both for the kinds of knowledge and perspectives such an education offers and because of the higher-end skills it develops.[14]

Employers have been saying this for a long time. Back in 1953, John McCaffrey, who was then president of International Harvester, stated that a business graduate's perspective tends to be too narrow, and therefore he "does not see over-all effects on the business." McCaffrey encouraged engineering and technical schools "to give a larger part in their courses to the liberal-arts subjects" because business leaders needed a "rounded education." In 1960, William Benton, a partner at the advertising firm credited with inventing the soap opera, admitted that as "a student at Yale forty years ago, I specialized in a mishmash labeled 'Finance'—to my everlasting regret." Business programs "too often are a waste—of time, money, and the priceless opportunity to prepare for successful careers." In contrast, a liberal arts education "is the best preparation to cope with the barrage of new ideas constantly clamoring for an executive's consideration." Students should take "concentrated doses of English, mathematics, the natural sciences, history, psychology, economics and the humanities," he concluded. To Benton, "the traditional liberal arts course is as practical as a cash register for a businessman. Indeed, even four years of Latin are more useful than a once-over-lightly course in production or merchandising."[15]

This leads to the second major weakness of the undergraduate business degree: it is less likely to foster the skills that employers value. In *Academically Adrift*, sociologists Richard Arum and Josipa Roksa found that students taking courses in the arts and sciences produce significantly greater gains in critical thinking (as measured by the Collegiate Learning Assessment, or CLA) than do business majors. They attribute the result to the fact that students in the sciences study the most hours and students in the humanities read and write the most.[16]

In their follow-up book, *Aspiring Adults Adrift*, Arum and Roksa acknowledge that the data is messy. First, students move between majors quite a bit. Second, a good part of the difference may have to do with differences between selective and less-selective institutions. Third, because of self-selection, less academically able students probably opt out of arts and sciences majors. Nonetheless, they again conclude, "students who majored in traditional liberal arts fields—social sciences, humanities, natural sciences, and math—demonstrated greater improvement on the CLA than did students who majored in business."[17]

Arum and Roksa's research suggests another reason why refocusing undergraduates on the liberal arts and sciences will improve student learning outcomes. One of *Academically Adrift*'s conclusions is that schools with a campus culture of achievement tend to produce better results. Presumably, as colleges once again gain clarity of purpose by abandoning the mission creep that has turned them into curricular shopping malls, campuses will again emphasize the core virtues of intellectual inquiry and academic achievement.

Because there is no reason to conclude that majoring in business leads to higher salaries, and because the liberal arts and sciences produce higher student learning outcomes and may lead to more satisfying careers, it is not unreasonable to argue that eliminating undergraduate business majors will improve students' earning potential and the nation's economy while providing better opportunities for college students.

The Virtues of College

The third, and *most important*, reason to abandon business majors is because business majors are antithetical to college education and unworthy of a college degree *even if* it could be proven that they produced higher salaries. College students ought to study the liberal arts and sciences because they provide the knowledge, skills, and virtues that are necessary both for preparing people to be effective citizens and leaders and productive participants in the workforce, as well as to further their own learning. While there may be utilitarian arguments for majoring in business, colleges must remain true to their own internal purposes.

American colleges have been exceptional in their desire to offer every student a liberal education. Today, many policy makers are asking whether the liberal arts are relevant for the twenty-first century. "The question is un-American," journalist Fareed Zakaria argued. It was America, after all, that democratized access to liberal education.[18] But increasingly, a liberal education is a luxury good. Even liberal arts colleges now market their programs as a "boutique" product for privileged students.[19]

Ultimately, then, the reason to abandon business degrees is because college is not for anything and everything. A college graduate ought to be a different kind of person than someone who did not attend college. The issue is not just skills, but character. It is not about being for or against business, but rather about protecting the specific kinds of education that a college degree should represent. A good college education offers access to the *knowledge* requisite to be a thoughtful interpreter of the world; fosters the *academic skills* necessary to develop meaningful interpretations on one's own; and cultivates *intellectual virtues*. In other words, college is defined by its content—by the kinds of things that one ought to think about.[20]

The business major supports those students who want a college degree without a college education. Philosopher Tal Brewer has written that the very notion of business school is an "oxymoron." The word *scholar* derives from the Greek word for leisure. Schools are places where people step aside from the world of need—from the world of business—to engage in reflection. Colleges, "devoted to discussion and thought unfolding under its own internal demands," cannot with integrity offer "training for the sort of life that has no place for such thought." Business schooling is "a *scholé* of the negation of *scholé*."[21]

Moreover, business is an activity that we engage in to achieve other goods. A college graduate must be educated to think about those goods thoughtfully and critically, especially because markets are cultural institutions, shaped by what we value. Even wages depend as much on cultural as on economic causes.[22] But the very existence of the business major teaches students that the end of business is business. In reality, each good or service has its own distinct purposes, practices, and virtues. To reduce this beautiful complexity to maximizing profit or creating efficient supply chains confuses means with ends. The end of farming is to produce healthy food. The end of building cars is to produce transportation. The end of medicine is health. In a market economy, farming and automobile production need to remain viable; farms and automobile companies don't exist primarily to enrich shareholders but instead to produce value for our society. Students need to think about the specific goods that they are producing—their social value, their history, and the ways in which they are part of a larger culture. In short, business people should not think of themselves as business people at all, but as people who offer services and goods, whether they be banking or medicine, farming or automobile manufacturing.[23]

Liberating colleges—and students—from undergraduate business majors will allow colleges to focus once again on what college is for. Today, as one critic writes, elite colleges "boast that they teach their students how to think, but all they mean is that they train them in the analytic and rhetorical skills that are necessary for success in business and the professions."[24] Ending undergraduate business programs may not alone solve this problem, but it will create the space to do so by eliminating the need for the arts and sciences to compete on business majors' terms and instead to concentrate on the specific goods and practices that they stand for.[25]

This is a fundamental problem that cannot be fixed simply by offering business degrees with a "liberal arts twist," as one news story put it, because, by treating business as an end in itself—by making it a major—we allow college students' self-formation to be shaped by the goods of business instead of the goods of a liberal education.[26] We must care about what students attend to during their time in college, and from this perspective undergraduate business majors are not just ineffective but unethical.[27] Undergraduate business programs are anti-intellectual in an institution whose purpose is intellectual. That is precisely why, at the end of the day, there is no justification for undergraduate business majors. They do not necessarily lead to higher salaries; they produce lower student learning outcomes; and ultimately they are in tension with the ethical and intellectual purposes of collegiate education.

In an era when high-stakes, complicated reforms are in the air, abandoning undergraduate business majors offers a simple but effective fix that colleges can undertake right away, and the benefits, for students, for colleges, and for society, will be significant. Perhaps it is indeed time to reform the American college.

Teaching

CHAPTER SEVEN

On Time and Experience

T HERE IS a trend in higher education to offer college credit for prior learning and demonstrated competence. Both approaches are intended to offer college students, especially nontraditional ones, faster paths to earning credits and degrees. They are contrasted—condescendingly—to most colleges' expectation that students spend a certain amount of time (which of course costs money) on their campuses. For example, in one of the highest profile speeches of his tenure as President Barack Obama's Secretary of Education, Arne Duncan advocated giving college credit for what students know instead of "seat time." President Obama also spoke in favor of competency-based programs in his proposals to reform higher education.[1] And despite criticizing some of the Obama administration's rules, Betsy DeVos, President Donald Trump's Secretary of Education, also voiced support for increasing federal support for alternative educational models.[2] In short, the desire to speed up degrees, and the corresponding lack of appreciation for the role of time, is shared by leaders in both of America's major political parties.

Competency-based education works by identifying the specifics things that someone needs to be able to learn or to do in order to earn a degree (or to pass a course), and then allowing students to move forward as soon as they have demonstrated that they have mastered the expectations. Prior learning programs enable students—especially older, returning students—to earn credit for what they have learned from work and other forms of experience.

Perhaps these approaches make sense in those vocational fields in which knowing the material is the only important outcome, where the skills are easily identified and the primary goal is certification. But in other fields—the liberal arts and sciences, but also many of the professions—this approach simply does not work. Instead, for most students, the experience of being in a physical classroom on a campus with other students and with faculty remains vital to what it means to get a college education. Indeed, for a college education to be effective in all its spheres—developing students' knowledge, skills, and virtues—we must respect, and therefore be willing to pay for, time.

Liberal Education

The goal of a liberal education is to transform a person by offering her or him serious and diverse intellectual experiences. As Edward Ayers, former president of the University of Richmond, put it, liberal education should be seen as experiential learning for the mind. It seeks not just to demonstrate a series of outputs but instead to offer a significant number of inputs. The quality of intellectual experiences—not just the mastery of competencies—is at the heart of a serious college education.[3] "College education," philosopher Gary Gutting writes, "is a proliferation of such possibilities: the beauty of mathematical discovery, the thrill of scientific understanding, the fascination of historical narrative, the mystery of theological speculation. We should judge teaching not by the amount of knowledge it passes on, but by the enduring excitement it generates."[4] In other words, traditional colleges offer students an education, not just certification.

A good liberal education is not just about learning to write well or to think critically, or any other specific outcome or competency. Instead, it is also about putting students into contexts in which they are exposed to new ideas and asked to chew on them and talk or write about them. One hopes that students will be disturbed and fascinated—and even thrilled—by what they learn. These kinds of experiences happen when students spend time interacting with professors and one another on campuses. Even if students have mastered the basic competencies, they should still take more classes, because liberal educators seek to ensure that students will have the intellectual experiences that make college education worthwhile.

It is hard to quantify the value and lasting influence of an experience. We know that the world is always interpreted, and these interpretations are shaped by the categories of thought that we use to make sense and to make meaning. A good education should offer experiences that reshape those categories so that our interpretations—in fact, the world itself—appears different to us before and after the educational process. Even better, a good education should provide us with the skills, categories, knowledge, and habits that make us not just interpreters but skilled, conscientious, thoughtful, and profound interpreters of our world.

In truth, there is an anti-intellectual tendency in the effort to award significant academic credit for nonacademic experiences. The competency-based approach is designed to eliminate the mediating role of teachers. Teachers, after all, can be quirky and different from one another, since each teacher is an expert but has a human—and, therefore, particular—relationship with her or his subject. But that is also why teachers matter. By caring about the material and about students, teachers create a connection between the two. They do not simply provide content but rather offer contexts for understanding.

By watching others care deeply, students start to see why what seems unrelated to them—what seems academic—can actually shape their relationship with the world. This kind of mediation is teaching at its best.

Competencies

The competency-based approach not only reduces the role of teachers, it risks treating knowledge of a subject as secondary to mastering the skills: as some have put it, it's not what you know that matters, but what you can do.[5] However, recent work on the brain has made clear that *to know* and *to do* cannot be disaggregated—facts become knowledge when our brains are engaged actively in learning them.[6] Skills, moreover, are often the means, not the end. For example, we may read books and write papers to become better critical thinkers and writers, or we may learn to think critically and write papers in order to understand books better. In the academy, at least, the latter should also be a priority.

Offering substantial credit for "prior learning," for experiences beyond the academy, by its very nature conflates categories. Education is not limited to schooling. The education of a human being happens through culture, through families, through churches; only a part of education happens through formal schooling.[7] Yet, these realms of life are different in their goals, in their criteria, and in their material. To recognize that people learn as much from life as they do from school is not an insult to formal schooling; it is a reality of living. To give credit for experiences that are not properly academic is to undermine the higher academic—that is, intellectual—purposes of formal higher education in the arts and sciences.

This is not to say that there is no role for identifying competencies in the arts and sciences. In fact, the American Historical Association undertook a "tuning" project to help history departments identify what history majors should be able to do and to demonstrate these skills to outside constituents, including employers.[8] Such an approach can improve teaching and help those outside the discipline understand the kinds of skills and intellectual habits that history majors develop, but these competencies cannot adequately represent the value of a liberal education or even of a single course.

For example, even if one could prove that a history major has met a set of competencies—like learning to think historically, write well, and analyze data—that is not enough to earn a history degree, since one of the most important parts of being a history major is learning about different times and places in new ways. History programs ask students to take classes on different eras and places with different professors because it is worth doing, even if students are "competent" historians. Demonstrating competence, therefore, is only *one* of the goals of the history major.

The same applies to other fields. In English, for example, is it enough to learn to read and analyze texts well? Or do we want students to spend time in classes where they engage in serious conversations about texts and where they have experiences that can inspire them to see the world differently? We hope students will be asked to take different courses and read different kinds of literature with different kinds of professors, because these experiences are as important as the competencies students develop on the way.

This is as true of general education. The goal of general education is not just to master competencies but also to expose students to different domains of knowledge and ways of thought. We thus cannot treat knowledge as incidental or epiphenomenal to college education. We do not want to teach students just "literacy" or "critical thinking." Instead, we want them to read, to enjoy, and to learn from actual literature, and not only from "literature" but from actual texts. To reduce literature to literacy misses the point entirely.

Skills are vital, of course. One cannot do history or chemistry or carpentry without them. They must be learned. No doubt they are often transferable, and thus have general value. Yet to evaluate a historian or a chemist on some set of generic skills, with no attention to knowledge or purpose, is muddled at best. It would be like evaluating guitar players on their manual dexterity, with no concern about what it means to be a guitar player or even to play particular songs. The dexterity gained in learning guitar cannot be alienated from the student's or the teacher's goal of producing specific kinds of music with a particular musical instrument. A student learning guitar seeks a particular kind of excellence.

Therefore, assessments of student learning must be designed in ways that are compatible with the purposes of college education. To measure student learning in ways that are abstracted from the life-world in which skills take on meaning, are practiced, and are developed would erode the ethical and intellectual purposes of a bachelor's degree. It would treat skills as ends, not as means to an end.

A Good College Education Takes Time

Efforts to make college faster, including competency-based education, ignore the simple fact that a good education takes time. It takes time to foster students' dispositions, or their virtues and habits. It is not enough that students demonstrate the ability, for example, to write a research paper. Students must come to think of intellectual inquiry as an end in itself, something that they cannot, and would not, avoid. They should seek not credits, grades, or competencies, but understanding.[9] Ideally, college students will approach graduation with a sense of sadness as well as accomplishment because they have come to love learning so much.

Class time is formative. It enables students to gain specific insights into the world under the mentorship of experts. Every course is a vista point over a landscape that allows students to see their world differently. This is by its very nature particular—particular to the teacher, the text, the material, and the student. These insights in turn form the lenses through which students view the world. They provide understanding, cultivate the imagination, and are the basis for asking new, better questions.

It also takes time to develop skills. To become skillful requires repetition, not single moments of demonstrated competence. For example, one can pass a driver's exam by cramming and taking written and skills-based tests. Yet that does not a driver make. A driver becomes a driver through repeated practice, until driving becomes something that one does skillfully. The same is true for learning intellectual skills.

Thus, it takes time to gain insights, to develop new dispositions or habits, and to master the skills necessary to achieve knowledge. Ideally, students shouldn't just learn skills and knowledge; they must become the kind of people who use their intellectual skills to seek knowledge, and to do that well, they need actual knowledge, actual vistas, to make sense of the world.

To defend time is not to defend the status quo. Class time must be *good* time—it must ensure that students engage their minds. Students cannot sit passively; professors must do much more than lecture. Classes must be small enough for real faculty-student interaction, and faculty members must demand of themselves and their peers they teach students all three things—knowledge, virtues, and skills. To make seat time good time requires, first, recognizing the value of seat time, and second, helping students use seat time to get off their seats and use their minds well. In other words, what matters is *time* more than seats.

Time matters, but the time must be good time in good communities oriented to the right ends. Any person who has been part of a community—a church, for example—knows how important time is for forming and educating human beings. One cannot become a church member by passing a set of competencies quickly and easily. One becomes a church member by changing, and this requires knowledge and a new set of dispositions, a new orientation. The same ought to be true for college graduates.

That is also why undergraduate colleges should not be integrated into the world, even as they prepare students for it. Some, including many policy makers, celebrate campuses that bring employers in, integrating the "real world" and the campus, but college and university campuses are places apart for a reason. They establish sites for reflection, something that is not easy to do in a world that places many demands on us. From this perspective, programs that emphasize speed and align themselves too closely with employer needs can never achieve the goals of a good college education because they cannot ensure that all college students have the opportunity to be, as philosopher Michael Oakeshott put it, "inhabitants of a place of learning."[10]

Finally, time matters because educating a human being requires mentors who form deep, meaningful, trusting, and *intellectual* relationships with their students.[11] These relationships matter at a practical level because they are correlated with student retention, but they ultimately matter because that is the way we human beings learn best. Our brains, cognitive scientists have discovered, set up barriers to learning that make it difficult to change our minds. Students—and faculty members too—need to feel able to open themselves up to risk in order to experience real learning. Good teaching and good student learning thus require that students have time to find intellectual mentors and to develop trusting relationships.[12]

No matter how we move forward, then, we will need to think about time as an asset rather than an impediment. We will need to find ways to provide students of all ages and backgrounds with time to devote to becoming educated. Already, students spend too little time on campus. Already, working adults lack the resources to take time away from their busy lives. To reduce students' time on campus would only make it more difficult for colleges and universities to offer a high-quality and meaningful education. Such efforts might increase access to college degrees, but not to the education that must accompany those degrees.

Fostering students' curiosity about the world requires that students be immersed for a part of their lives in an environment that treats intellectual inquiry—not demonstrating competence—as the highest goal. Competency-based education can improve the quality of college education by helping colleges and disciplines identify some of the specific skills and knowledge that they want their graduates to exhibit, but it will always be just a part of the overall picture. A good college education must also offer intellectual experiences not available elsewhere, which can change a life and last a lifetime. This requires time. This is why competency-based education and awarding credit for prior learning will not be a disruptive game changer for most college campuses, despite many reformers' efforts and policy makers' hopes.

CHAPTER EIGHT

On Online Education

THERE HAS BEEN MUCH talk of the "online revolution" in higher education. While there is a place for online education, some boosters anticipate its displacing the traditional campus altogether.[1] A close reading of their arguments, however, makes clear that many share what might be called the "individualist fallacy," both in their understanding of how students learn and how professors teach.

Individualism has a long, noble heritage in American history. From the "age of the self-made man" onward, we have valued those who pull themselves up by their own bootstraps. But, as investor Warren Buffett has made clear, even the most successful individuals depend heavily on the cultural, economic, legal, political, and social contexts in which they act.[2] This is as true for Buffett as it is for other so-called self-made men, such as Bill Gates, and it is certainly true for students.

Many advocates of online learning, however, ignore this simple point. One economist proclaimed that being on campus is primarily useful for "making friends, partying, drinking, and having sex." Journalist and author Anya Kamenetz celebrated the day when individuals would be liberated from the constraints of physical campuses, while Gates anticipated in 2010 that "five years from now on the Web for free you'll be able to find the best lectures in the world. It will be better than any single university."[3]

There is nothing new about these predictions that technology will displace the human interactions that are at the heart of physical campuses. Inventor Thomas Edison was so excited by films that he proclaimed in 1913 that "books will soon be obsolete in the schools." Others anticipated that radio would soon make college education available cheaply to all. After World War II, the Ford Foundation was confident that television sets would do what films and radio had failed to do. In each case, colleges experimented, businesses partnered, foundations invested, and policy makers praised and hoped—and yet the college campus and the face-to-face classroom survived.[4]

Like their predecessors in the early twentieth century, today's advocates of online higher education forget the importance of *institutional culture* in shaping how people learn. College is about more than accessing information; it's about developing an attitude toward knowledge. There is a difference between being on a campus with other students and teachers committed to learning and sitting at home. Learning, like religion, is a social experience. Context matters. No matter how much we might learn about God and our obligations from the Web, it is by going to church and being surrounded by other congregants engaged in similar questions, under the guidance of a thoughtful, caring pastor, that we really change. Conversion is social, whether in churches or colleges.

Like all adults, students will pursue many activities during their time on campus, but what distinguishes a college is that it embodies ideals distinct from the rest of students' lives. If we take college seriously, we need people to spend time in such places so that they will leave different from when they entered.

Some argue that large lecture courses make a mockery of the above claims. Admittedly, in a better world, there would be no large lecture courses. Still, this argument misleads for several reasons. First, it generalizes from one kind of course, ignoring the smaller classes in which students interact closely with one another and their professors. Second, it dismisses the energy of being in a classroom, even a large one, with real people, when compared to being on our own. Even in large classes, good teachers push their students to think by asking probing questions, modeling curiosity, and adapting to the needs of the class.

Finally, it disregards the importance of the broader campus context in which all classes, large and small, take place. The goal of bringing students to campus for several years is to immerse them in an environment in which learning is the highest value, something online programs, no matter how interactive, cannot simulate. Real learning is hard; it requires students to trust one another and their teachers. In other words, it depends on relationships. This is particularly important for the liberal arts and sciences. Students learn most on campuses where learning is valued and expectations are high.[5] We want students to be in an environment that cultivates intellectual virtues. If anything, we need to pay more attention to campus culture because it matters so much.

This does not mean that we should reject technology when it can further learning, such as software that can help diagnose students' specific stumbling blocks. But computers will never replace the inspiring, often unexpected conversations that happen among students and between students and teachers on campuses. Because computers are not interpretive moral beings, they cannot evaluate assignments in which students are asked to reflect on complicated ideas or come up with new ones, especially concerning moral questions. Fundamentally, computers cannot cultivate curiosity because machines are not curious.

Technology is a tool, not an end in itself. As the computer scientist Jaron Lanier has written in *You Are Not a Gadget*, computers exist to support human endeavors, not the other way around. Many techno-utopists proclaim that computers are becoming smarter, more human, but Lanier wonders whether that is because we tend to reduce our human horizons to interact with our machines. This certainly is one of the dangers of online higher education.[6] At the heart of education are human relationships. Whether in the liberal arts and sciences or in professional fields, good teachers seek to develop specific human capabilities. These capabilities might be different in the liberal arts and sciences than in engineering or carpentry or cooking, but they share a common commitment to human development.[7]

Developing human beings depends on trust. Cognitive scientists have found that students do not really open themselves up to being changed absent trusting relationships.[8] Indeed, when education scholar Parker Palmer surveyed students about their most influential teachers, he discovered that a teacher's impact depended less on pedagogical technique than human presence: "Listening to those [students'] stories, it becomes impossible to claim that all good teachers use similar techniques: some lecture nonstop and others speak very little; some stay close to their material and others loose the imagination; some teach with the carrot and others with the stick." What united the stories was students' recognition that "good teachers share one trait: a strong sense of personal identity infuses their work." That identity is what Parker calls the teacher's "heart," the place where the teacher connects the material to herself and to the student.[9] In short, if we care about changing students' hearts and minds, we need to invest in physical environments where students and professors can interact in meaningful ways.

The individualist fallacy applies not just to online advocates' understanding of student learning but also to their conception of what makes great teachers and scholars. The economist Richard Vedder, for example, echoes Gates in his hope that someday there will be a Wikipedia University, or that the Gates Foundation will start a university in which a few "star professors" are paid to teach thousands of students across the nation and the world.[10] Of course, this has been happening since the invention of cassette tapes that offer "the great courses." This is hardly innovative, nor does it a college education make.

Vedder ignores how star professors become great. How do they know what to teach and to write? Their success, like Buffett's, is social: they converse with and read and rely on the work of hundreds, even thousands, of other scholars. Read their articles and books, listen to their lectures, and you can discern how deeply influenced by and how dependent they are on the work of their peers. In short, there would be no star professors absent an academy of scholars committed to research. Take away the professors, and many online schools will teach material that is out of date or inaccurate or, worse, hand control over to entities that are not interested in promoting the truth—from textbook companies seeking to maximize sales to coal and pharmaceutical companies offering their own curricula for "free."

Advocates of online education argue that the campus experience is unavailable or irrelevant to older students. These claims insult older learners, who may want, and certainly are as deserving of, a liberal education as are traditionally aged students. No doubt, colleges need to find ways to help older students return to campus, including thinking about how courses are scheduled and programs are organized. We also need public policies to support older students who want a college education, including financial aid and other kinds of aid, such as child care. Any American who wishes to go to college and is qualified should be offered an opportunity at the real thing. Supporters of online education are correct that traditional institutions can do a better job making themselves accessible to nontraditional students. However, when supporters of online education proclaim that nontraditional students are too practical or too old to want or to receive a traditional college education, they demonstrate a lack of respect for both the students and for colleges' purposes.

We will expand online higher education, if for no other reason than because wealthy foundations like Gates's and ambitious for-profit entities are putting their money and power behind it. For students pursuing clearly defined vocational programs rather than a college education, online programs may allow opportunities they would otherwise have had to forgo. But online higher education will never replace, much less replicate, what happens on college campuses. Even if we expand online, therefore, we still must deepen our commitment to those institutions that cultivate a love of learning in their students, focus on the arts and sciences, and produce the knowledge that online and offline teaching requires.

CHAPTER NINE

On Critical Thinking

EVERYWHERE WE turn these days, we hear that colleges are not teaching "critical thinking." Employers want critical thinkers, but they cannot find them. Entire books conclude that colleges have failed to increase students' critical thinking. Nicholas Lemann, former dean of Columbia's School of Journalism, urges colleges to foreground method, not content, in their general education programs. Many high-profile reformers agree that professors too often focus on "content" over "skills," thus failing to prepare students to be learners.[1]

Advocates of critical thinking contrast thinking critically with learning knowledge. College professors, they proclaim, teach a bunch of stuff (facts, dates, formulae) that students don't need and won't use. Instead, students need to have intellectual and cognitive skills. As *New York Times* columnist Thomas Friedman has proclaimed, "the world doesn't care anymore what you know" but "what you can do."[2]

There are two problems with this perspective. First, it is fundamentally anti-intellectual. It presumes that the material colleges teach—the arts and sciences—does not matter, when, in fact, this is the very reason colleges exist. Second, these claims are wrong. Cognitive science demonstrates that if we want critical thinkers, we need to ensure that they have knowledge. Thinking cannot be separated from knowledge. Instead, critical thinking is learning to use our knowledge. The most effective critical thinkers, then, are those who learn history or physics. The stuff we learn about matters.

In many ways, the turn to skills is a defensive response. At a time when the humanities, in particular, are under attack, what better way to defend the humanities' "useless knowledge" than by demonstrating that these are means to a larger end: critical thinking? However, one must acknowledge that these defenses reflect the capitulation of academics to utilitarian and pragmatic pressures.[3] Lacking a convincing argument for the knowledge that anthropologists or historians have to offer, they instead proclaim that history and anthropology will serve employers' needs better than will other fields. But if that's the case, why does one really need to know anything about anthropology or history? Why should colleges hire anthropologists or historians instead of professors of critical thinking?[4]

This is not an abstract question. When we turn from higher education to the K–12 system, we see that the focus on skills over knowledge has transformed the curriculum. Increasingly, especially under the Common Core State Standards, students devote their energies to learning skills, but they may not learn as much history or civics or science.[5] Therefore, in contrast to the anti-intellectual rhetoric of many reformers, critical thinking must be defended because it encourages students to gain more insight from the arts and sciences.

To understand why, let's return to an earlier example (see chapter 7): imagine your employer provided you with a manual dexterity class in which you learned to move your fingers about effectively. Now imagine that you came to a guitar teacher and asked for credit. Certainly, guitar players need to have manual dexterity, but the guitar teacher would wonder why you deserved credit. Learning dexterity absent actually playing guitar is not particularly valuable. It certainly does not mean that one can play guitar, nor that one has understood guitar or embraced the purpose of studying guitar. It's a meaningless skill from the perspective of a guitar teacher. The same is true about critical thinking in the arts and sciences. Critical thinking is not enough and on its own, isolated from meaningful subject matter, is unimportant.[6]

How, then, should colleges and universities understand skills? They should see them *in relation* to the goods of liberal education. This means that skills should be developed in the context of reading and writing about literature or history or engaging in scientific inquiry. Collegians care about the question, Critical thinking to what end? Colleges' goal should be to encourage students and professors to gain as much insight from studying history or economics or physics or chemistry as possible. In other words, critical thinking is not a self-standing goal independent of the larger purpose of a college education; instead, it should be intimately connected to developing students' intellectual virtues, habits, and knowledge.[7]

Critical Thinking

What do we mean by critical thinking? Often, advocates of critical thinking portray it as an independent set of cognitive skills that are easily transferable. They advocate critical thinkers because employers and political leaders want people who can solve complex problems, but they do not care much about what students think about. Colleges do. As one skeptic of "critical thinking" has written, "if we describe college courses mainly as delivery mechanisms for skills to please a future employer, if we imply that history, literature, and linguistics are more or less interchangeable 'content' that convey the same mental tools, we oversimplify the intellectual complexity that makes a university education worthwhile in the first place."[8]

At a deeper, more profound level, critical thinking can be seen as a disciplined activity on its own terms. Indeed, one might understand it as a revival of the trivium of grammar, rhetoric, and logic. These were the original liberal arts, and the term *arts* meant *techné*, or techniques (think of artisans) to analyze texts and problems. In this sense, critical thinking can be understood as a deep activity, one that requires the development of new habits of mind. It is not something we can get without extensive study and practice. The skills that we apply to problems and texts, the capacity to understand arguments, to make sense of their strengths and weaknesses, and to offer new and creative solutions is gained by consistent and constant study over years.[9]

Yet even this more profound understanding of critical thinking cannot be separated from learning subject matter in the arts and sciences. We can only think critically about things about which we have knowledge, and we can only make use of facts if we know how to think about them. As James Lang writes in *Small Teaching: Everyday Lessons from the Science of Learning*, "knowledge is foundational: we won't have the structures in place to do deep thinking if we haven't spent time mastering a body of knowledge related to that thinking." For example, the answer one might expect to the question, Why do we have global warming? would be very different from a student with background knowledge in chemistry or public policy or economics than from someone who had not studied these subjects. An ignorant person may well conclude, in a great demonstration of "critical thinking," that the earth is getting warmer because the sun is getting hotter. It makes sense, it's reasonable, and it is also wrong. The same is true for almost any sophisticated question.

This happens. When students graduating from Harvard College and ninth graders at Cambridge Rindge and Latin School were asked about the seasons, they demonstrated amazing levels of "critical thinking," but they did not have the background knowledge to get the correct answer. Many believed that the seasons were caused by the Earth's orbit. Some offered complicated responses that exhibited the students' "critical thinking" and creativity. But they were wrong. If they had remembered that the seasons had something to do with the Earth's tilted axis, they could have reasoned themselves to the correct answer.[10]

One has to know things to answer things. This is true even in the age of Google. If one looks up something online, one needs to know a lot of background information to make sense of the definition and explanation—and given how unreliable many online sources are, without that background knowledge, one might be led astray. But perhaps most surprising, those with more knowledge can learn more when they look something up on Google. That's because if they already have background knowledge, they can add to it the new information and insights from what they are learning. This means that someone who understands political science and has some knowledge of how parties function will learn more from an online news story about elections than someone lacking that knowledge. Those who know more learn more than those who do not.[11]

In other words, intellectual skills and knowledge are not two distinct things. They must work together to produce critical thinkers. Put more baldly, despite all the rhetoric, there is no such thing as critical thinking in general. People think critically when they know how to use knowledge to solve problems and to generate new knowledge. At the heart of critical thinking, therefore, must be a resolute rejection of "critical thinking" in favor of enabling students to study and to master bodies of knowledge with which they can think critically—whether organic chemistry or the causes and consequences of the Boxer Rebellion. If we emphasize generic skills over learning specific subject matter, we will graduate worse critical thinkers. Paradoxically, to improve critical thinking, despite what the reformers and skeptics say, we need to abandon the idea that we can teach generic thinking skills and instead allow students to devote more time to learning "useless knowledge."[12]

General Education Matters

We often presume that thinking critically in one domain leads to thinking critically in all domains. There is some truth to this. Someone who embodies the intellectual virtues will have a desire to understand the world's problems and thus to educate her- or himself about them. Someone with a high capacity to use language or numbers will be able to address various kinds of questions wherever they arise, including in the office. Yet there are limits to these claims. For example, when mathematicians are asked why their students need to learn math they will never use, they argue that advanced subjects like calculus or linear algebra make students better critical thinkers. But it's not clear that this is the case. Even among the top math performers on the SAT, only a minority scored equally well in the verbal section. Andrew Hacker discovered the same was true when he did a study of his own students at Queens College, New York. Doing well in math did not necessarily lead to doing well in history because each subject made distinct demands on students' thinking and relied on different disciplinary skills and background knowledge. To be good in math, one should study math; to be good in history, one needs to study history.[13]

We cannot expect that students will be experts in every subject. Still, we can learn something about why knowledge matters by examining the difference between experts and nonexperts. Scholars have concluded that experts are not smarter in general, nor do they have some generic critical thinking skills. Instead, experts draw on background knowledge unavailable to nonexperts. Moreover, many of their skills are domain specific—meaning that better doctors may not be better architects, too. What makes an architect better at planning buildings is not her critical thinking but knowledge of how buildings are designed. What makes a doctor better at promoting health and reducing sickness is not critical thinking but his knowledge of medicine. Experts, in other words, rely on knowledge and domain-specific skills.[14]

Why do we need knowledge to be critical thinkers? The reason actually is simple. To make sense of any reading (or lecture, or documentary, or TED talk) about anything, we draw on what we know. No text is isolated from the world. The more that is in our head, the more we can make meaning of what we are reading, whether it's a poem, a scientific study, or a news story in print, online, or on TV. When we assign students reading tests, except in the earliest years of their childhood, students are forced to use their background knowledge to understand them. Students who have more knowledge will, therefore, do better. This is true at a basic level—our minds map words and associations, so the richer our vocabulary and the more that we have read, the easier decoding is. It is also true at a higher level. We may be able to decode "the White House said today," but we can understand it only if we know that the White House is the place where the president of the United States lives. As psychology professor Daniel Willingham writes, good readers need more than technical reading skills; they require "broad knowledge about the world."[15] Unlike math assessments, where skills and content overlap, reading tests do not actually test generic reading skills; they are as much about how much you know.

If the above is true, then general education programs may be the most important thing colleges offer to undergraduates. There's a reason why general education programs (or core curricula) are the only requirements college establish for *every* student. Whether one majors in philosophy or marketing, one has to meet the same general education requirements. It's the one thing that the college considers essential to having a bachelor's degree. That is because the general education requirements are designed to offer students access to background skills and knowledge in the liberal arts and sciences. That knowledge defines a college education. It contextualizes the specific skills and knowledge that one learns in one's major.[16]

Proclaiming the general education program to be the most important program on campus goes against common sense. Most students try to get their general education requirements "out of the way." Professors want to teach upper-division specialized courses in their research areas and do not agree on what would make up the content of a shared curriculum anyway. Administrators rely on large general education classes, often taught by non-tenure-track professors, to subsidize smaller more specialized courses. And, to pragmatic policy makers, who want to offer more degrees faster and cheaper, general education courses just seem like a waste of time and money. Thus many states offer students incentives to earn their general education credits in high school, either by taking high school classes for college credit, by attending junior college courses, or by earning Advanced Placement credit.[17]

In response to policy makers' skepticism, some college leaders have urged revising general education programs to focus on skills (such as critical thinking or analysis) over subject matter. Generic skills are touted in part because they are easier to assess. Professors are expected to show that by, for example, teaching the American Revolution, they are *really* teaching critical thinking and analysis. Which of course they are. One cannot learn about the Revolution without analyzing sources and thinking critically about different interpretations. Yet the purpose of the class is not "critical thinking" but helping students be more insightful about the American Revolution. That insight will be part of students' intellectual toolkits as they enter the world. It will help inform how they make sense of other questions and provide the basis for new knowledge, not just about American history, but about politics. Achieving that goal requires professors who care intensely about the material. Rather than focusing on generic skills, then, we should find ways to encourage innovative teaching that helps students learn the material better.

Critics of knowledge contrast "critical thinking" with memorizing isolated facts. It is a straw man argument. Isolated facts are not knowledge. They become knowledge when we interpret them and use them and make them our own. The straw man works because many students spend too much time in school memorizing isolated facts to pass exams, and many professors confuse the memorization of facts with knowledge. Knowledge requires using facts to answer questions in order to develop lasting insight. This is not to say that memorization is never necessary. Your mind needs to have facts in its memory to do higher-order thinking, and a certain amount of "recall" is useful to learning material. But memorization should be used strategically as a means to the larger end of gaining a real understanding of course material.

The next step is to ask students to use the facts to build knowledge themselves. Professors must design their courses so that students engage the subject matter from multiple perspectives, reflect on what they have learned and its implications, and use their knowledge to produce new knowledge and deeper insights. This can be done through discussions, labs, reading, various kinds of writing, small group work, as well as effective and strategic use of lectures. Good teachers do not ask students to think critically in some abstract way, but instead employ strategies that enable students to internalize the subject matter and use it. We should encourage professors to adopt strategies that will, in the words of one set of scholars, "make it stick."[18]

Knowledge is vital for equality. Students from less-privileged backgrounds often lack the background cultural and scientific literacy to do advanced coursework. Whether in the K–12 system or higher education, this creates inequalities in outcomes. A student cannot understand a text if he lacks the information required to make meaning of it. This is as true for *Tales of a Fourth Grade Nothing* as it is for *House on Mango Street* or *A Tale of Two Cities*. Standardized tests often try to pretend otherwise by having students read fictional and nonfictional texts that they have not confronted before. But to make sense, for example, of the Rev. Martin Luther King Jr.'s "Letter from a Birmingham Jail," one needs background information about American history, race, and Christianity.[19]

Knowledge is also important for the future of our democracy. Thomas Jefferson understood that because the people are "the ultimate guardians of their own liberty," Americans should support public schools, "to diffuse knowledge more generally through the mass of the people."[20] A more contemporary study raises concerns about "truth decay" among American citizens today. At a time when the internet offers fake news and wildly divergent accounts of events and policies, citizens must have the background knowledge and intellectual skills to evaluate new claims and facts and to make reasonable judgments about the truthfulness of what they read or hear. As one commentator put it, if we elevate critical thinking without teaching students knowledge, "the sky becomes the limit as to what one might think and whether it has any foundation in reality."[21]

If colleges really care about critical thinking, they need to teach students subject matter in the arts and sciences. This means overcoming the dichotomy between thinking and facts. We think with facts, and we use intellectual skills or methods, often disciplinary-specific ones, to interpret those facts. In turn, the knowledge we gain becomes the foundation for new knowledge when we are faced with new problems or information. A critical thinker is not one who has learned "critical thinking," but one who has thought critically about various subjects. An educated person has a storehouse of cultural and scientific literacy to draw on when she is seeking to make sense of the world around her. To improve critical thinking, then, we must provide students more opportunities to study the arts and sciences. We must emphasize knowledge, not "critical thinking."

Scholarship

CHAPTER TEN

On the PhD

M OST OF this book has focused on undergraduate collegiate education, whether it takes place in independent colleges or at larger universities. Yet it is worth taking a moment to think about the purpose of graduate education. The PhD, unlike the bachelor's degree, is a vocational degree. It prepares scholars to enter careers in the arts and sciences, whether in colleges and universities, government, or the private sector. Just as law school prepares lawyers and medical school prepares doctors, so a PhD program prepares academics. No less than undergraduate education, then, graduate programs in the arts and sciences must orient their practices around their specific ends.

Instead, there seems to be a trend to treat the PhD as a general degree rather than one devoted to specific ends, especially in the humanities, where there are too few tenure-track positions to accommodate all qualified doctoral candidates. A task force of the Modern Language Association, for example, encouraged English and other language and literature departments to prepare PhD candidates for careers outside the university.[1] The American Historical Association, the professional association for historians, has been having similar conversations. In their important, humane contribution to the conversation, "No More Plan B," the American Historical Association's Anthony Grafton and James Grossman argued that, at a time when the employment market for history PhDs is dismal, historians with PhDs have high-level skills that should be recognized by employers.[2] Since then, the American Historical Association has launched a series of initiatives to promote career diversity for history PhDs. Some evidence suggests, not surprisingly, that PhDs in the humanities are already thriving in the private sector.[3] In *The Graduate School Mess* (2015), English professor Leonard Cassuto writes that "the notion that graduate school is specialized training ground for future professors has been untenable for more than two generations. . . . This old-fashioned training leads graduate students to a narrowly specialized course of study that is at best impractical and at worst destructive. It teaches them to want and expect the wrong things."[4]

These conversations reflect concerned academic leaders' efforts to find ways to deal with the human cost of declining faculty positions in the humanities (and even, one might add, in the natural sciences).[5] These proposals are controversial because, to their detractors, they turn graduate education in the humanities into job training. At a time when the humanities are threatened and when many policy makers are emphasizing narrowly vocational goals over a broad general education, this is not an unreasonable concern. But graduate education in the humanities should not be defended because it prepares people for a wide range of jobs. That's not what brings students to graduate school. Students enter graduate school because they love their subjects. They have had good teachers who have inspired them to see the world in new ways. They have learned to ask the kinds of questions that only the humanities can answer. They have been converted.

We therefore should not treat the humanities PhD like a high-end professional credential—an alternative to the MBA. When we do so, we corrupt what graduate study in the arts and sciences is for. Unlike the undergraduate major, which is intended as broad preparation for life, the graduate degree is designed for those who wish to engage in deep study to enter professional work in the humanities. Instead, we should think of graduate education in the humanities as akin to ministerial education. We must prepare students not just with the knowledge required to understand their field, but with the skills necessary to carry out their ministry in the different places to which they might be called. By imagining ministers instead of MBAs, we might be able to find a language that makes it possible to reform graduate education without giving in to vocationalism.

Yet before reforming graduate education, we must not forget the primary issue faced by the humanities (as well as other fields): the structural problems that plague colleges and universities—namely, the shifts away from tenure-track hiring and from the liberal arts and sciences.

On the demand side, we need to expand the number of tenure-line positions in the humanities across the nation and resist the deprofessionalization of professors.[6] On the supply side, we need to recognize that we are overproducing. One reason that we do not curtail supply, however, is that research institutions want the cheap teaching labor that graduate students provide. Absent graduate programs, professors would have to teach more students and classes or universities would need to hire more professors. The first option is unpopular with professors, the second with administrators. This is not to deny that individual faculty members invest their hearts and souls in mentoring graduate students, but instead that universities have underinvested in tenure-line faculty. As Marc Bousquet pointed out, in some ways graduate students are the waste products of the system: their value to the university is used up when they receive their degree.[7]

A focus on structural solutions would help those called to the humanities find professorships. If the jobs are not there, however, the answer may not be to continue to overproduce PhDs and market them to private employers, but to reduce production. Unlike the undergraduate humanities major, which is part of a general liberal education and needs no vocational justification, the graduate program is designed to lead students to meaningful work.

Humanities as a Calling

Students come to graduate school in the humanities because of their intellectual passion for their subjects. Universities must respect what brings them to campus. PhD students are not budding entrepreneurs; they are ministers committed to spreading the gospel of the humanities. We must prepare them for the ministry they came to undertake, whether in educational institutions, government, or other organizations.

For most humanities PhDs, the primary work will be teaching. Humanities PhDs teach at the secondary and college levels, but humanities programs have been relatively disengaged from the task of preparing teachers. Although we have allowed teacher preparation to take place almost entirely within education schools, there are many reasons why liberal arts and sciences programs should be more involved in preparing teachers.[8] Moreover, the cost of the split between secondary teachers and professors has been significant. In the history discipline, the division between professors and other historians has devalued the daily ministry of most historians, led to an overemphasis on scholarship, and denied secondary school teachers opportunities to engage in the life of the discipline.[9]

Even if most humanities graduates will teach, we should not denigrate scholarship. Too many policy makers and commentators have suggested that humanities research does not matter. It matters greatly, both in the public sphere and in the classroom. To sustain scholarly inquiry, we need scholars around the country and the world engaged in research and capable of critically assessing one another's work. We need to ensure that humanities graduates wherever they are employed—in K–12 schools, museums, local societies, media, universities, businesses, government—have the space, time, and respect to engage in scholarship and be part of the conversation.

Reforming Graduate Education

If it is deemed necessary to reform graduate humanities education, we must always keep in mind that we are preparing humanities ministers. Keeping this conviction first and foremost in mind opens up alternative ways to reimagine graduate education.

We might, in addition to or instead of the PhD, offer a doctorate of humanities (like the JD or MD), a four-year program that would offer a solid academic education, require a significant work of scholarship in the form of a publication-worthy thesis, and also provide practical skills to help apprentice humanists enter the humanities fields at various levels in different kinds of organizations. The doctorate of humanities could be interdisciplinary or field-specific, as different institutions and programs and the needs of scholarship determine appropriate.[10]

To get a sense of what this might look like, consider divinity programs. No less than PhDs in the arts and sciences, divinity students are driven by their mission to understand and share their faith. In addition to the PhD, however, divinity schools offer robust Masters of Divinity programs, which are shorter and oriented toward the academic preparation of practicing ministers. At Harvard Divinity School, for example, the M-Div is a three-year degree combining academic knowledge (such as history and theology) with ministerial methods and field placement.[11]

Princeton Theological Seminary in New Jersey also offers both a PhD and a three-year M-Div. Students are expected to take coursework in biblical studies, history, and theology. But academic work is insufficient. There is also a "practical theology" component to help ministerial candidates learn how to preach, educate, and perform pastoral care. Finally, the program requires "field education." The degree prepares its graduates "for the diverse ministries of congregational leadership, for graduate study in theology and related disciplines, for various types of chaplaincy, for mission work at home and abroad, and for other forms of church vocation."[12] Without reducing or diminishing academic preparation, candidates are taught to use their academic knowledge to carry out the very important work that they will undertake as ministers.

A similar combination of academic and practical education could prepare graduate students in the humanities better for their jobs as teachers (including classes on pedagogy) and for work in the public, nonprofit, or private sectors. Such a degree would be more portable and, as a result, would reduce the human and financial cost for those who cannot find professorships or choose other careers.

There is no reason to believe that such a degree would reduce the quality of humanities scholarship or supplant the PhD. A four-year doctoral degree with a serious research component should prepare graduates for research as well as other kinds of work. After all, most ministers do not need PhDs, nor do most lawyers or MDs. They need an education that enables them to undertake their daily work with thoughtfulness, provides the skills to make them effective practitioners, and gives them the ability to engage in scholarship.

In the past, such proposals have faced challenges, the most important of which has been one of prestige. Compared to the PhD, applied doctorates, such as the PsyD in psychology and the EdD in education, tend to be considered second tier. Yet as early as the 1930s, reformers promoted doctors of arts degrees that would take less time and be less research-focused than the PhD. In the 1960s, the Doctor of Arts took off, in part because of the high demand for college teachers. As demand fell, however, colleges and universities started to expect a PhD for their new professors.[13]

On the other hand, MDs and JDs have valuable degrees. Medical schools and law schools prepare their graduates for successful careers in medicine and law, including in research. What unites these successful degrees is that they are not general degrees but are specialized training for specific professions. The same must be true for graduate education in the arts and sciences. In the humanities, this means that we cannot defend the PhD as a portable degree like the MBA. Instead, the goal should be to prepare humanists to work in the humanities, whether or not in colleges and universities. Moreover, an alternative to the PhD might offer students who wish to continue to study the humanities after graduate school for personal or professional reasons, but not necessarily to become professors, the opportunity to do so.

In conclusion, we need to continue to move forward on two fronts. The crisis of doctoral education is, to a large extent, a crisis of the university. It is not about supply, but demand. We therefore must prioritize the need for more tenure-track hiring in the liberal arts and sciences. That is the most pressing problem facing graduate education in the humanities, because the primary purpose of graduate education in the humanities is to prepare future scholars for teaching and research. Nonetheless, there is a good case to be made that graduate education in the humanities could be more expansive, not because we need to bow down to the anti-intellectual forces reshaping higher education, but because we can better prepare graduates for the diverse ministries that they could serve.

CHAPTER ELEVEN

On Research

TODAY, THE value of academic research, especially in the humanities and social sciences, is being questioned. In 2014, the Republican majority in the House of Representatives proposed cutting science funding for social science research and eliminating *all* funding for the National Endowment for the Humanities and the National Endowment for the Arts.[1] *New York Times* columnist Nicholas Kristof has accused faculty of engaging in specialized research disconnected from the interests of the reading public and policy makers, spurring a broad conversation about whether or not professors engage in the public sphere.[2]

There is no doubt that academics have a responsibility to engage public debates. In many ways, the academy is the critical conscience of a democratic society. It houses experts who use their knowledge to enhance the public's understanding of vital issues. Academic freedom ensures that scholars are able to use their hard-won expertise to inform questions of public importance.

Yet the value of academic research cannot and should not be measured, as some seem to suggest, simply by how many readers a journal article or academic monograph reaches. The purpose of academic scholarship is to engage in disciplinary inquiry—to further scholarly conversations. Such work will never be accessible to the general public since it works at the boundaries of knowledge and takes a certain amount of prior knowledge and expertise for granted (see chapter 12). Because academic research is specialized and takes place on the boundaries of what is known, it requires a community of experts. Disciplines form the communities of inquiry that enable academic research to take place. These communities require a critical mass of scholars to evaluate new work and to develop new knowledge.

Academics cannot read the work of all other academics. As a historian, for example, I rarely read and cannot truly understand publications in medical journals, or journals in chemistry or physics or other fields in which I lack the necessary knowledge of the specialized literature. I never doubt the value of these journals, however, for encouraging new ideas and practices in medicine, or chemistry, or physics. Whether in the natural and physical sciences or the humanities and social sciences, most academic work is by definition inaccessible to the uninitiated. This is not a bad thing. In the discipline of history, for example, I would worry if the primary criterion for the importance of a piece of academic scholarship was the number of its nonacademic readers. If academic history relied primarily on popular readers, most history (and the history of most people) would never get written.[3]

Again, this is true not just for the humanities or social sciences, as is often implied in public conversations about academic research. It is also true of the natural sciences. Basic research in all fields is vital for innovation.[4] The value of a particular piece of scholarship—whether measured in the number of readers, the impact on knowledge, or new products—cannot be known *a priori*. Every academic researcher is an entrepreneur, every book or article a start-up.[5]

Can the humanities produce "inventions" like the natural sciences? Even if our only understanding of invention is a technological product, the humanities have value. Linguistic scholars, drawing on ideas dating back to ancient Sanskrit grammarians, developed the tools of modern grammar that made it possible to invent computer programming languages.[6] And when we include new insights into culture, insights that transform our relationship with the world around us, then the humanities have a direct impact on our public lives.

Perhaps nowhere was this made clearer than in the US Supreme Court's decision that marriage is a fundamental right under the US Constitution. The court's decision, written by Justice Anthony Kennedy, upheld the historical significance of marriage and recognized the sanctity of the intimate relationships marriage makes possible.[7]

Early in his decision, Justice Kennedy cited three historians' works: Nancy Cott's *Public Vows: A History of Marriage and the Nation*, Stephanie Coontz's *Marriage, A History*, and Hendrik Hartog's *Man and Wife in America*.[8] These scholars' insights—their "inventions" of historical understanding—did not take place in a vacuum. They were the result of countless doctoral dissertations and "useless" journal articles. Cott, Coontz, and Hartog relied on and contributed to a vibrant community of scholars who, over the past few decades, sought to make sense of the history of American families. Scholars formed intellectual networks and new journals. They criticized each other's work and refined their understanding. They debated each other in print and at conferences. Over time, slowly and painstakingly, they taught us that American family life has a history, that the ways in which husbands and wives and parents and children relate to one another, and the legal and cultural contexts that shape those relations, have changed over time. Like everything else, families are part of culture.

In short, the Supreme Court relied on the very academic infrastructure for research that is now being undermined by public defunding and efforts to make colleges and universities more focused on workforce training. That academic infrastructure is threatened by efforts, such as those undertaken by Gov. Scott Walker in Wisconsin, to weaken the tenure and shared governance protections that sustain academic freedom and to emphasize vocational applications over basic research.[9]

For Justice Kennedy, scholars' "new insights have strengthened, not weakened, the institution of marriage." Historians have demonstrated how marriage, once a way to organize family resources or a method by which men exercised governance over their dependents, gave way in the wake of the American Revolution to something more egalitarian and more affectionate. In fact, our ideal of marriage as a relationship between two loving people deeply committed to each other was reinforced and popularized by the American Revolution, which challenged inherited ideas of inequality not just in politics but throughout society.

Historians, of course, did not make this happen on their own. Were it not for all the same-sex couples who dared to come out of the closet, all the organizers who built a movement, all the people who brought cases in the first place, and the lawyers who supported them, the issue would not have come before the Court. But if it were not for scholars of marriage, Justice Kennedy may not have had the knowledge before him to reach his decision. The value of basic research in the humanities cannot be denied. We need to reinvest in our research infrastructure so that we can continue to generate insights that will help us make sense of our most pressing public questions. Basic research in the humanities, it turns out, has a tangible social impact.

Similar claims can be made for the natural sciences. Many of the most useful inventions and breakthroughs in the sciences have emerged from basic research. Even the internet and the personal computer depended on government-funded academic research, which in time inspired both corporations and entrepreneurs to invest in the technologies that have generated immense wealth and transformed American society.[10]

Most small businesses fail, but that does not lead Americans to question the value of entrepreneurship. They should have the same attitude toward scholarship: most articles and books may not have a dramatic impact on the field or the public, but we cannot know which ones will. That's why we need to encourage start-ups and encourage creativity throughout the academy, just as we do in the economy.

The measure of success also has to be related to the "markets" that academic research serves. In the case of medical research, it is fair to ask whether research produces new knowledge that improves medical outcomes. In the case of such fields as history, then, we must ask whether academic research informs history's practitioners. The primary places where history is practiced, of course, is in schools. We must ask whether the curriculum offered in history courses at all levels—from elementary school to graduate school—is shaped by scholarship. Similarly, we should ask whether museums and historical societies offer interpretations influenced by academic research. If so, the case is made: historical outcomes have been improved, just as good medical research improves medicine's outcomes.

We must accept that the very nature of scholarship, whether in the humanities or the sciences, whether in medicine or religion, requires an expert, and therefore a limited, community of inquiry. Most academic work will always remain inaccessible to outsiders. A more sophisticated understanding of the value of academic research, and especially basic research in all fields, therefore helps us recognize not only the contribution scholarship makes to the public good but also how it does so.

CHAPTER TWELVE

On Academic Writing

O N   F E B R U A R Y   11,   2016,   a   team   of   scientists announced that it had recorded the sound made by two black holes colliding. Despite all the noise in the universe, the scientists' sensitive equipment found evidence of ripples in space-time, a core element in Albert Einstein's general theory of relativity. It was an amazing testament both to the power of the human imagination and to the daily work of basic scientific research. It took decades of painstaking effort and the commitment of scientists who spent their careers seeking to understand something most of us did not even know was being studied. One of those scholars, the Caltech physicist Kip Thorne, commented in the *New York Times*: "It's as though we had only seen the ocean's surface on a calm day but had never seen it roiled in a storm, with crashing waves."[1]

Intrigued by his remark, I looked up some of Thorne's scholarly articles. I have a PhD in history, but I was almost a geology major, and I've always appreciated scientific research. Yet I must admit, I could not make sense of his scholarly writing. It was filled with jargon and formulae.

Was that my fault? Was it the fault of Thorne and his coauthors? Was it, as Steven Pinker wrote, because academic writing stinks?[2] Or is it in the nature of scholarship to be challenging to the uninitiated because academics write at the edges of what is known? My own understanding of physics is far, far—light years perhaps—away from that of Thorne and his colleagues. And yet I am thankful for all of their work.

It has become a trope, a joke perhaps, to comment on how bad academic writing is. Thus, in the *Chronicle of Higher Education*, two critics launched the now-standard critique of academic writing:

> The transmission of our ideas is routinely hampered—understandably, given academe's publication, evaluation, and tenure conditions—by a great deal of peer-oriented jargon. As a result, the most exciting ideas, hard-won insights, and relevant hypotheses end up clothed in language that only specialists can understand. Academe's publication structure then exacerbates the segregation by

corralling this rich, important set of ideas within a tiny niche readership—in costly book-distribution contexts or expensive academic journals behind digital paywalls.[3]

Yes, some academic writing is more abstruse than it needs to be. No doubt, scholarship should not be hidden behind expensive paywalls. And, yes, academics, like all people, are shaped by the conditions of their employment. But the story is more complicated. Many critics rightly accuse academics of too rarely writing for the broader public. In doing so, however, those critics often confuse two different projects that have been distinct, and in tension with each other, since ancient times—participating in the public sphere (the domain of rhetoric) and seeking truth (the domain of philosophy). Each has its own ends, and thus distinct practices and virtues.

Rhetoric is interested in persuasion. Rhetoricians, therefore, have been primarily concerned with how to engage a public audience effectively. Public writing begins and ends with the public. Public essays require a "hook." They must derive their relevance from something au courant— often in a world of fast-moving news cycles. Good public writing must avoid scholars' tendency to "bury the lede."[4]

Yet there is a risk when we mistakenly assume that public and scholarly writing are the same thing—that one is good and clear and the other is needlessly complex. Critics often blame academics for overusing verbiage that is meaningless to the general public.[5] But jargon and complexity have their place. One need only ask whether theoretical physicists would have been able to achieve their insights if each of them had to write for lay readers like me instead of for each other. Of course not. There is jargon, and then there is jargon. In my own field of history, shared references to specific scholars, concepts, or schools of historiography can open up worlds of meaning economically. It allows us to focus on our shared task: scholarly inquiry.

Do scholars sometimes hide behind jargon? Of course. Can jargon mask emptiness? Yes. Do scholars sometimes use jargon when more accessible language is available? No doubt. Does jargon primarily serve the needs of tenure and promotion? Sometimes. Should academics write as clearly as they can? Yes. There is good academic writing and bad, just as there is good public writing and bad. But can we do away with jargon? Not if by jargon we mean scholarship that uninitiated readers simply cannot— because they do not have the knowledge to—understand. Indeed, to do so would make it impossible for scholarship to achieve its goals.

Plato mocked rhetoric. He believed that rhetoric, because it taught people to speak with the public, could never get out of the cave of shadows. Truth and goodness required leaving the ordinary world behind, emerging into the sun, and trying, however imperfectly, to get a sense of its beauty. The philosopher would never be able to return to the cave; indeed, he or she would have to be forced to do so for the good of everyone else, Plato famously argued in the *Republic*. But philosophers, having seen truth, will struggle to speak with people who remain enamored by shadows. Worse, the people will distrust them. The people will accuse them of attacking their idols. The philosopher could end up, as did Plato's mentor, Socrates, dead.

That was an extreme response to the question of the relationship between the public sphere and truth, but it speaks to a real problem. The public is not composed of philosophers. The public has its idols and wants them to be respected even if, from an academic perspective, they are just shadows. Yet in a democracy, one cannot imagine the public as nothing more than ignorant or impassioned. One must also recognize the majesty of the people, and acknowledge that democracy is the aspiration that we ordinary people, as citizens, can govern ourselves. Plato was no democrat. We are.

Democratic deliberation needs philosophy, because deliberation that relies on falsehood will lead to disaster. To gain truth, Plato was right: we need to allow philosophers to pursue it even when it is unpopular. We need to permit scholars to study human evolution or global warming. We need to be able to tell the truth about history, not because doing so is joyful but because it is how we can come to terms with our present condition. As James Baldwin wrote in 1965, it is only "in great pain and terror [that] one begins to assess the history which has placed one where one is and formed one's point of view."[6]

So, yes, scholars must engage the public. In doing so, however, they must respect the integrity of public conversations, which have their own traditions and icons, heroes and villains. "The nation," Ernest Renan wrote in 1882, "is a soul" sustained by "a rich legacy of memories."[7] Public conversations, like academic ones, rely on the shared reference points of a common culture. Public rhetoric requires starting where we as a people are and then taking us where the speaker or writer believes we need to be. It is a democratic practice.

It is very hard to engage in rhetoric and philosophy at the same time. That was something that the ancient Roman statesman Cicero understood. He recognized that many people shared Aristophanes' depiction of philosophers in his play *The Clouds*. Philosophers were lost in airy, arcane pursuits that had no bearing on the needs, aspirations, and lives of most citizens. Yet, Cicero responded in *The Ideal Orator,* however funny it is to insult philosophers for being inaccessible, that only takes us so far. The real problem is that rhetorical and philosophical activity are fundamentally different: "The procedures of oratory lie within everyone's reach, and are concerned with everyday experience and with human nature and speech." Scholarly inquiry, on the other hand, "draws as a rule upon abstruse and hidden sources." In philosophy, "the highest achievement is precisely that which is most remote from what the uninitiated can understand and perceive, whereas in oratory it is the worst possible fault to deviate from the ordinary mode of speaking and the generally accepted way of looking at things."[8]

Ancient writers and Renaissance humanists both struggled with how to bring rhetoric and philosophy together. They mocked writing that they believed lacked beauty. They wondered how the insights of philosophy might be made useful to public life. They hoped that there was an alternative to, in Cicero's words, the philosopher's "inarticulate wisdom" and the uninformed citizen's "babbling stupidity." Effective speech without wisdom was no better than wisdom that remained in the clouds.

That this is a centuries-old problem should give us pause when we echo Aristophanes and treat academic writing as nothing more than drivel.[9] Basic research in the arts and sciences is the source of wisdom, and that wisdom needs to be shared. There are in all disciplines scholars who fit Cicero's definition of the ideal orator, combining eloquence with wisdom. Yet Cicero recognized that the philosophical pursuit of truth requires different things than public engagement, which is a different kind of activity. We do neither academics nor the public any service when we conflate the two. Indeed, doing so is a categorical mistake.

We want physicists who write for each other. I appreciate that, at conferences and in academic papers, they have challenged each other's conclusions and, in doing so, have pushed forward the boundaries of knowledge. Yet I am also grateful for my scientist friends who posted on social media links to videos and essays in which scientists explained, in terms that I could understand, why it was so significant that they had heard black holes colliding.

I enjoyed physicist Lawrence Krauss's clear articulation of why a citizen like me—who could never understand an academic paper in physics—should continue to support investing oodles of money in basic research: "By exploring processes near the event horizon, or by observing gravitational waves from the early universe, we may learn more about the beginning of the universe itself, or even the possible existence of other universes." This matters: "Every child has wondered at some time where we came from and how we got here. That we can try and answer such questions by building devices like LIGO to peer out into the cosmos stands as a testament to the persistent curiosity and ingenuity of humankind—the qualities that we should most celebrate about being human."[10]

I appreciate the scientists who have taken time to write for readers like me about the importance of hearing ripples in space-time. But I am also thankful for the many scientists who spend most of their time talking to each other. Instead of writing for me, they devoted their efforts to producing inaccessible scholarship that, over time, produced public insights of profound beauty.

On the Future

THE UNDERLYING premise of this book is that America's colleges and universities are adrift because they are being asked to do too much and are being pulled in multiple directions. I believe that this is because reformers, shaped by their utilitarian or pragmatic ideals, are undermining the virtues of college education. In a sense, then, this book makes a conservative argument, in the best sense of the word. My goal is to protect colleges' and universities' academic purposes and the practices that sustain them. Colleges and universities should be places devoted to intellectual inquiry in the liberal arts and sciences, both through teaching and through research.

A good liberal education is not useless. College graduates who have cultivated the intellectual virtues and developed knowledge and skills through serious engagement with the arts and sciences will not only lead richer lives but will also contribute their capacities to civic and economic institutions. That may be why, despite skepticism among many policy makers and parents, business leaders consistently recommend a liberal education, and economists argue that a liberal education produces spillover effects that prepare people for economic success. It's not just skills that matter; what people learn matters, too.

As the provost and chief academic officer for the New School in New York City put it: "The capacity to understand the constraints and opportunities that are presented during times of transformation is key. This requires insight, perspective, self-reflection, and an entrepreneurial sensibility—all qualities taught in liberal-arts education. The ability to recognize the political, social, historical, and philosophical implications of contemporary experience is not only the hallmark of a liberal-arts education but also the trick of life-long learning."[1] In other words, it is extremely valuable to be able to place the immediate problems one faces into the broader contexts made available by the methods and knowledge fostered by the arts and sciences. As surprising as it may be, a liberal education is most useful and practical when it remains true to itself.

Although there is still time to save our colleges and universities from misguided reforms, we must start by refusing to idealize the past. Anyone who reads the history of higher education knows that our colleges and universities have never been devoted solely to one good. They have always been, and will most probably remain, institutions that contain the contradictory aspirations of policy makers, administrators, professors, students, and citizens.[2] Yet what distinguishes colleges and universities from other institutions in our society is their commitment to the value of intellectual inquiry in the arts and sciences. This is what sets a college or university apart and defines it. It is its essence. One can have a college or university without programs in business, education, engineering, or health, but not without the liberal arts and sciences.

The United States, unlike many other nations, has a long tradition of encouraging college students to pursue liberal education and of funding basic research in the arts and sciences. Today, this tradition seems less secure.[3] But, lest we lose hope, it's worth remembering that Americans have before and may once again recognize the value of liberal education. We have also before and may also once again recognize that basic research in the arts and sciences yields ideas and inventions vital to our national well-being. As President Ronald Reagan said,

> The remarkable thing is that although basic research does not begin with a particular practical goal, when you look at the results over the years, it ends up being one of the most practical things government does. For example, government-sponsored basic research produced the first laser. Today, less than three decades later, lasers are used

in everything from microsurgery to the transmission of immense volumes of information and may contribute to our Strategic Defense Initiative that promises to make ballistic missiles obsolete.[4]

We need to distinguish the specific ends of four-year colleges from other forms of useful postsecondary education. Four-year colleges cannot do everything; that's why we need to fund technical and vocational schools, community colleges, and apprenticeship programs. There is no doubt that every American needs to have a basic liberal education in the arts and sciences. That's one of the major purposes of K–12 education. The purpose of four-year colleges, then, is to educate those who wish to continue to study the arts and sciences. But there are lots of ways to be educated; the goal should not be to diminish the importance of job training. At some point, we all need jobs. For many Americans, a bachelor's degree in the arts and sciences is great preparation because so many jobs require diverse skills and the capacity to learn, and because a good liberal education also prepares people to pursue graduate and professional degrees.

But we should not oversell the bachelor's degree. It is a general degree. Despite our prejudices, there's no reason why someone with a bachelor's degree should not seek vocational training either in a graduate professional school (such as education, law, or medicine) *or* through a technical or vocational program. Doing so does not take away from the value of the liberal education that he or she received in college. Similarly, there's no reason why persons with technical or vocational training should not, if they wish, go to college and receive a liberal education at any point in their lives. The two kinds of education are distinct. Just as liberal education has its purposes, virtues, and practices, so too do most occupations and professions. We do ourselves an injustice when we conflate liberal college education and vocational and technical education or presume that one is prior to the other. Worse, we send thousands of young people to college, making them study subjects that they care little about and making it harder for colleges to stay true to *their* mission.

If a college education is more than a degree, we must attend to its specific virtues. Being adrift has its dangers, because the tides and currents exert their own force. As our colleges and universities have floated away from their mooring, they have been pushed by the sea into a new port, where a college degree is primarily for getting ahead. It provides job training and certifies to employers that graduates are employable. In many cases, its worth is determined by the salaries of graduates. The new port values the production of degrees, but it is less concerned with the content of the education.[5]

There is still time to save our colleges from misguided reforms. We must refuse, however, to turn the clock back to some past time. To be conservative is not to be rigid. The goal is to protect what matters and reform what needs reforming in order to achieve the right ends. If we truly believe in the academic purposes of college education, we must make our institutions places that they have never been. In this sense, there is much work ahead for reformers.

We need to enable students of all ages and backgrounds to take the time to enter the academy's walls, regardless of where they are in their lives. Too often today's reformers pretend that adult learners don't need or want a liberal education. That is insulting both to adult learners and to colleges and universities. We need colleges to be accessible to students of both traditional and nontraditional backgrounds. Too often, getting into college and paying for it reinforces America's inequalities rather than challenging them.[6] In fact, colleges and universities are themselves guilty of marketing the value of their degrees over the quality of their education. This can be seen both in their efforts to recruit students with pleasures external to education (such as climbing walls) and in the unseemly race to celebrate the prestige of their diplomas over the intellectual experiences available on their campuses.

To make these institutions places that they never were, we need to increase public funding, so that students are able to pursue their education without worrying about their loans, and so that professors can pursue knowledge rather than seek industry support for their work. Despite what many Americans think, the primary driver of rising tuition at most public universities, where most Americans go to college, is the erosion of state support.[7] Because many Americans and policy makers pretend that the purpose of college is to get a degree that raises one's earnings (a private benefit) rather than an education that serves society (a public good), they wonder, why fund it? And if the primary purpose of research is to design products for industry (a private good) rather than to seek truth (a public good), why fund it? Thus, legislators and taxpayers have transferred the burden of paying for college from taxpayers to individuals and of research to investors.[8]

In addition to funding, we must think seriously about what happens on college campuses. We know that colleges that set high academic standards and focus on the arts and sciences post the largest gains in student learning. We can start, then, by exploring ways to make campuses better places for students to engage in intellectual inquiry. We need, for example, higher walls between campuses and the "real world" in order to insulate students and professors from utilitarian and pragmatic pressures.

We must also find ways to encourage and reward better teaching. We should rethink the structure and content of the curriculum. For example, we must scale back programs, such as undergraduate business, technical, and health programs, that do not align with colleges' academic purposes and thus weaken efforts to cultivate an academic environment. Yet this is not enough. We must be willing to ask hard questions about how to organize the curriculum and even how to deliver it. As a start, we must revise general education programs so that students are offered meaningful and sustained intellectual experiences in the arts and sciences, not just a "check-box curriculum."[9]

Colleges should also strengthen academic freedom, tenure, and shared governance so that professors can hold colleges and universities accountable to academic values and priorities.[10] The virtues and practices of academic life are oriented around its end: to cultivate a community of scholars committed to the production and sharing of knowledge. By ensuring that academics play a role in shaping institutions' priorities and curricula, shared governance limits the intrusion of nonacademic values on scholarship and teaching. Critics have suggested that new technologies and economic necessity have made shared governance outdated. In reality, there is nothing new about the pressures scholars are facing from institutional managers, politicians, and business interests. Today, shared governance is more necessary than ever if colleges and universities are to maintain their academic purposes.

None of the above reforms is easily met. All require creative and challenging reform of institutional structures, funding, professional practices, and curricula. We need reformers who care about what colleges and universities ought to be and want to help them become what they never quite were. Unfortunately, this is not the direction that American reformers are taking. Thus, let's pretend for a moment that the arguments of the so-called reformers are right: colleges and universities are about to face disruptive innovation from a disgruntled public, unhappy employers and policy makers, and new technologies. Let's assume, moreover, that the many books that document the sad commercialization of higher education are also correct: colleges and universities are becoming more like businesses, students are becoming more like consumers, and research is becoming more like product development. Perhaps we are indeed witnessing, as one scholar has put it, "the last professors."[11]

These worries are most likely misplaced; the worst-case scenarios probably will not happen. Traditional undergraduate liberal education will survive. When the fads pass, students will continue to go to college campuses, where they will spend several years of their lives in a residential learning community before going out to seek a job or professional training. Professors, not computers, will remain the primary mediators between knowledge and students. Moreover, since much of the hostility to professors emerged as part of the broader post-1960s culture wars, it is possible that, with changing generations, support for academics and the liberal arts and sciences will revive. Already there are bipartisan efforts to articulate the value of the humanities and the liberal arts at a time when they are at risk in colleges—and even high schools—across the nation.[12]

Unfortunately, as this book argues, the most prominent and popular reforms today threaten academic life; some are downright hostile to it. In such a context, academics ought to imagine ways to nurture academic life beyond the college or university.

The Academy and the University

For the past century, the academy has found a home in the college and the university—they have been co-constitutive.

Rising prices, declining state support, neoliberal assumptions about the value of education and how to fund it, and the growing number of students seeking higher education for vocational purposes have placed pressure on colleges and universities as academic institutions. As one researcher has noted, universities are increasingly devoting more resources and higher salaries to "scholars whose careers are the least defined by the university's original academic mission."[13] This is a particularly acute problem for the humanities. As another observer writes, "the basic infrastructure of humanistic knowledge is being dissected: libraries cannot buy enough new books, journals and university presses are under intense financial pressure . . . departments are being closed, fewer and fewer faculty are being hired on the tenure track."[14] For a time, one could rest assured that even if the percentage of American undergraduates majoring in the humanities was declining, the overall number of majors was not.[15] More recent analyses suggest, however, that we are now seeing declining numbers of students choosing to major in the humanities, even at elite schools.[16]

The liberal arts and sciences, once the heart of the university, are now marginalized as students choose professional or STEM degrees. Expanding numbers of students come to college primarily to get a degree, not for a liberal education. In response, colleges have expanded their offerings to serve a broader set of interests and needs.[17] Our institutions have become shopping malls without focus and purpose.[18] As the famous and influential University of California president Clark Kerr wrote back in 1963, the modern university is no longer defined by its ends, but is better understood as a "multiversity"—"a whole series of communities and activities held together by a common name, a common governing board, and related purposes." Indeed, he continued, the multiversity is "a city of infinite variety."[19]

In reality, this variety is evidence of drift; colleges and universities are trying to do too much for too many people and are thus unable to achieve coherence. With new technologies thrown into the mix, it is conceivable that in a couple decades, America's colleges and universities will no longer be academic institutions at all.

In such a context, it is vital that academics start thinking about ways in which to promote academic research and teaching outside of colleges and universities. For-profit corporations are not an option since they commodify knowledge and consider students to be consumers, violating academics' core ethical commitments. Instead, something else must be found. We have seen in journalism what happens when profit seeking trumps the professional autonomy of journalists.[20] Similarly, in medicine, commercial interests threaten the professional integrity and autonomy of doctors.[21] The same threat exists for the academic profession if professors cannot resist managerial and political efforts to promote the bottom line over the public good. With this threat in mind, I offer here sketches of four potential ways forward.

Four Options for an Academy
beyond the Multiversity

Under what I call the "Adam Smith option," academics could be authorized to teach by colleges and universities or disciplinary organizations but would effectively be independent operators—like many music teachers—in a market context. In *The Wealth of Nations*, Smith criticized universities for permitting academics to be lazy and ineffective. He argued that faculty members should earn their keep through the quality of their lectures.[22] His critique has limits; it does not, for example, account for the intrinsic motives that inspire teachers to work long hours and to do their best despite poor pay and external rewards.[23] Nonetheless, Smith's model is one way forward. For this model to work, local colleges and universities or local or state chapters of disciplines would need to determine which teachers are to be authorized to teach for credit, much as Suzuki or Montessori teachers are certified today. Colleges, depending on their missions, could set standards for different kinds of degrees and allow students to seek out their own teachers. This would reduce administrative costs, as colleges would no longer need large staffs.

A second option is for academics to rely more heavily on philanthropy in order to create teaching and research centers oriented around specific themes or goals. Again, disciplines may have to take the lead in seeking out philanthropy in order to establish endowed institutions that can and are willing to promote scholarly research. Potentially, tenure, peer review, and other academic practices could be preserved and scholarly institutions could offer "badges" and other forms of credentialing distinct from the bachelor's degree. On the other hand, academics would have to accept more influence from philanthropy. Philanthropists would most likely endow institutions compatible with their own values and interests. Like the Brookings Institution, the Urban Institute, and the American Enterprise Institute, these would promote and sustain research. This is, however, nothing new: the modern research university also owes its emergence in part to elite philanthropists.[24]

A third option is for professors either to take back the college and university or to start new ones. This will be hard. Despite some efforts, faculty have never managed to achieve control over their institutions but only, at most, shared governance, in which boards of trustees and their appointed administrators continue to dominate the overall coordination. Unionization will help, since faculty can protect some of their values via collective bargaining. A better alternative would be to imagine new, truly small liberal arts and sciences institutions, which would educate small batches of students. We live in a society that appreciates the craft production of everything from beer and coffee to clothing. There is no reason we cannot have micro-colleges, which engage in "artisanal teaching" and promote "close learning."[25] Assuming these institutions could overcome the administrative burden of accreditation and be affordable (by focusing solely on academics and avoiding the various other services that drive up college administrative costs), they could be run like char-ter schools and win political support from policy makers on the right and left. The benefit would be the creation of smaller, more intimate schools, perhaps closer to ear-lier American colleges, whose origins can be found in the seventeenth- and eighteenth-century dissenting acade-mies established in England as alternatives to Oxford and Cambridge.[26]

A fourth option is the "yoga option." In this scenario, academics become alternative practitioners who abandon entirely colleges and universities that have become too corrupt or vocational to promote the academic enter-prise. Academics would have to earn their keep by taking on students or earning research grants from independent institutions or the government. This is not inconceivable, however. In communities across America, music instruc-tors, yoga instructors, masseuses, herbalists, and all kinds of alternative-knowledge teachers and producers earn a living. These teachers are certified, apprentice under local masters, have networks in which they engage in continu-ing professional development, as well as online and print media to which they contribute and from which they learn about their own fields. Moreover, they have found people who want their services.

Academics could do the same. Again, disciplines may have to take on new credentialing services and reimagine themselves to serve academic practitioners not housed in colleges or universities. Local communities of historians or political scientists or chemists could meet regularly, as well as be connected intellectually and professionally through their disciplinary organizations. The existing disciplines may, in fact, become more interdisciplinary under the broader umbrellas of the human and natural sciences. People would teach locally, and academics could join together to offer arts and sciences within a common practice, much as different alternative practitioners do today.[27] Indeed, one could walk down the street, and next to the yoga and karate studios might be a *studium generale*. As do other alternative teachers, academics would also take on apprentices in anticipation that they, too, would become credentialed—perhaps through writing peer-reviewed papers for journals, or books—in order to teach. Academics and their students would develop their own local and translocal networks of knowledge outside colleges and universities.

There is significant historical precedent for the yoga approach. The natural sciences developed in large part from amateur scientific societies in civil society well before the sciences gained the prestige and popularity to become part of the college curriculum. During the eighteenth-century Enlightenment, salons and coffeehouses served as nodes in a trans-Atlantic network of political, cultural, and scientific knowledge production and circulation. Thus, two of the core pillars of the modern academy—the Enlightenment pursuit of truth and the methods of science—emerged out of civil society.[28]

Adult students, in particular, may seek out the services of independent academic practitioners. There is a long history not only of colleges and universities engaging adult students but also of adults pursuing their own liberal education through voluntary associations, churches, and other institutions. Adults, no less than young people, need access to the liberal arts and sciences in order to reflect on the purpose and meaning of their personal, civic, and working lives.[29]

Challenges

Each of the four possibilities sketched above is intended primarily to provoke thought and to clarify what is at stake in our discussions of the future of American college education. Each of them would face real challenges. The most important challenge from a teaching perspective would be to ensure that students still find themselves in "communities of learning" that replicate what residential campuses offer.[30] The research challenge would be how to fund important scholarship in the arts and sciences without colleges and universities providing the infrastructure—the funding, the scholarly publishers, the equipment, the libraries, and the labs. In the natural sciences, especially, the capital costs for cutting-edge research are substantial, and private and public funding sources would want to ensure accountability. Yet, just as the National Endowment for the Arts makes public grants to artists both within and beyond the university, public humanities and science funding could be offered to academics or communities of academics outside colleges and universities.

Another challenge would be prestige. Today, the authority of educational credentialing is owned by colleges and universities. If academics abandon the university, or if the university abandons academics, then academics—like doctors seeking legitimate authority in the nineteenth century or practitioners of alternative medicine seeking legitimate authority in relation to MDs today—would have to fight to reestablish the legitimacy of their knowledge and modes of research and teaching.

No matter how we proceed, advocates of the arts and sciences will need, like churches following disestablishment, to find a way to bring in people who do not know that they need to be converted. Colleges offer students a liberal education that many students neither want nor believe they need. That may be why small liberal arts colleges are struggling today, and some are shutting down or starting vocational programs. But many students also go to college open to being educated. They discover how a good education can transform their understanding of the world. Academics will need to ensure that all people—younger and older, richer and poorer—are offered the time and opportunity to see their world anew and to take their new knowledge and skills with them into the workforce, their private lives, and the public life of our democracy.

These options may not work; certainly they are not ideal. Colleges and universities have been supportive partners of the academy, and it would be a shame and a loss if they had to part ways. On the other hand, as American colleges and universities become more vocational and less academic in their orientation, academics may need to find new ways to live out their distinct calling. The academy is not the university; the university has simply been a home for academics. College and university education in our country is increasingly not academic: it is vocational; it is commercial; it is becoming anti-intellectual; and, more and more, it is offering standardized products that seek to train and certify rather than to educate people. In turn, an increasing proportion of academics, especially in the humanities, have become adjuncts, marginalized by colleges' and universities' growing emphasis on producing technical workers.

The ideas offered above would all build on the core commitments of the academy and the tradition of seeing the academy as a community of independent scholars joined together to produce and share knowledge. Increasingly, however, colleges and universities claim to own the knowledge academics produce, as do for-profit vendors who treat knowledge as proprietary. To academics, each teacher is both an independent scholar working with her or his students and on her or his research and also a citizen committed to sharing her or his insights with the world as part of a larger community of inquiry.

If the academy seeks to create spaces for academic life beyond the college and university, it will have to be creative. Academic knowledge and intellectual virtues matter too much to society for Americans to allow the changing university to determine the fate of academic teaching and research. If and when academics can no longer call the university a home, they (we, since I am one) will need to build new shelters in civil society. The academic commitment to liberal education and scholarship may have to find new ways of expressing itself, but one way or another, it will.

On Talking with Students

I BEGAN THIS book with a story of a student. I want to share another: One day, a freshman who was taking my introductory course in US history came to my office. He was fulfilling his general education requirements, including a course on music. As we talked, it became clear to me that he was a first-generation college student. His parents and siblings were working in the fields, but he had been given the opportunity to come to Western Washington University. He felt guilty about his privilege. His family was working hard while he was learning about music and the American Revolution. Was he being selfish? Shouldn't he be helping them?

I urged him to stay. My family, too, immigrated, I told him. I did not grow up under the same circumstances as he did, but my parents sacrificed much to send me to college. For them, and for me, it was an opportunity for social and economic mobility. If his parents were like mine, they would want him to be in school. He was doing the right thing by his family.

We cried as he struggled. He was having a tough time in school. He wanted to help his family, and how would learning about music or early American history help? I tried to make the case. Yes, it's a privilege to be able to study music and history. Try to appreciate the privilege. You are getting a liberal education, and that education will serve you long after you have received your degree. A good education provides a foundation for success in all spheres of life. What a wonderful thing. Embrace it.

These arguments, I could tell, were too abstract for him. I did not want him to drop out, but that was a very real possibility and, I fear, may have been his ultimate choice. Was he right that students like him don't have the time or money for classes in music and history? Was he right that such classes are not useful for someone like him? That's what policy makers assume when they complain of the time it takes students to earn all their general education requirements.

And yet, here before me was a first-generation student. Was he not as deserving and in need of a liberal college education as an elite student at one of the nation's top colleges? His education would prepare him to be a citizen of our shared democracy. With his education, he would contribute to our economic, social, and cultural well-being. A good education would expand his horizons as he developed deeper understandings of the world we shared. That was not a waste; it was a blessing.

But he felt it was wasteful. He felt it was a luxury. He felt it was irrelevant. He was not hostile to what I said, but my words did not speak to him, even as we shared a close moment. I think that he knew that I cared for him, but I'm not sure that he believed me. The experience humbled me. I recognize that it takes a lot of faith for students, especially if they're worried about their families and their futures, to put their trust in an education that seems impractical.

Thus, colleges face large challenges. They must not just respond to elite policy makers and reformers hostile to their liberal purposes but also find ways to reach those students who think that liberal education is not for them, that it's a privilege, or that it's useless. This is not just about first-generation students. I have had many privileged students, too, who approach their education instrumentally, seeking good grades, perhaps, but not an education.

———————

I ADMIT THAT college is not for everyone and everything, and it cannot satisfy—nor should it—all the competing ambitions of potential students. No matter how good the campus culture, no matter how committed the professors, not every student will be intellectually engaged. But college is nonetheless for certain things, and every student who is qualified and steps onto a college campus deserves those things, whether they are rich or poor; white, brown, or black; younger or older; and whether they know they want it or not.

Students are under intense pressure to go to college. My hope is that, in the precious little time that most students spend in college, they also receive an education that can enrich their individual lives and serve them in their roles as friends and neighbors, parents and partners, citizens and members of the workforce. Although it can be a hard case to make, it's not an impossible one. Students have open minds. They care about the world and want to make it a better place. When I teach my students about the ends of liberal education, they are surprised that they have not heard about them before. Many come to appreciate liberal education's importance.

Liberal education, of course, is not the only kind of education that a person needs, and college is not the only place where one learns. But liberal education, I believe, is important to a person's intellectual and moral development. There are many good reasons for liberal education, from the personal to the civic to the economic, and this book, among many others, has articulated some of them. Students need to be made aware of these reasons, but the goal of college education is even more ambitious. Colleges should aspire to cultivate the intellectual virtues, so that learning is not just something one does for a grade, or for credit, or for a degree, but for the joy of gaining insight into the human and natural worlds.

A good liberal education can inspire people to keep learning. It prepares graduates to answer all kinds of questions more deeply, whatever they go on to do with their lives. That's why, when someone says to me, "I'm not really using my education," I respond, "you're using it every time you think, everywhere you think."

ACKNOWLEDGMENTS

THIS BOOK REFLECTS a decade of learning about the state of higher education, the shifting landscape of education policy, and the ambitions of reformers past and present. I have long been interested in the history and practice of education, but, like so many professors, I started paying attention to higher education—reading about it, writing about it—in response to the forces that were reshaping it in ways that threatened the things to which I had dedicated my life. In other words, I did not choose to become involved with the study of higher education; I had to get involved to understand what was happening to America's colleges and universities.

I accrued many debts as I pursued my learning and shared my thoughts. Doug Lederman, coeditor and cofounder of *Inside Higher Ed*, published many of my writings, but he also encouraged me to offer deeper analyses. He reminded me that my job is not just to vent about what I dislike and praise what I like, but rather to do what historians do best and offer context and more detailed explanations. Doug edited my submissions to

Inside Higher Ed, and in doing so tutored me. I am deeply indebted to his time and support.

Greg Britton at Johns Hopkins University Press was enthusiastic about this book from the get-go. Knowing his critical acumen, I was excited to work with him. He has been a partner throughout, helping me refine my argument but also urging me to hold fast against temptations to tack too much one way or the other. His intellect, his support, and his guidance have made this book much better. Barbara Lamb did an excellent job editing the manuscript for production.

Ed Ayers first suggested that I write a book on higher education during an early morning coffee at a meeting in DC. I had not thought about it, and his remark started me down the path that became this book. James Grossman, the American Historical Association's executive director, offered consistent encouragement and criticism. His engagement inspired me to keep on thinking about higher education reform and to offer answers, however tentative, to questions we share about the university's future.

During my tenure at the Institute for Advanced Studies in Culture at the University of Virginia (during the 2014/15 and 2015/16 academic years), I benefited from conversations with the institute's resident scholars. Chuck Mathewes was a consistent critic and advocate, as a colleague and mentor should be. At the institute, I had the good luck to cross paths with Chad Wellmon. We discovered quickly that we were thinking about similar things. Both through conversations with Chad and by reading his published work, I have gained an immeasurably richer understanding of higher education's past, present, and potential future.

I have the good fortune to work at a college that has thoughtful, devoted professors and administrators across campus. One of the benefits of campus service is that one learns about the work of one's colleagues and benefits from their insights and experiences. I have profound respect for the care and commitment that my colleagues, in their own disciplines, demonstrate daily. My campus is filled with thoughtful teacher-scholars. I have learned much about how colleges work, don't work, and perhaps should work from colleagues and friends with whom I have worked on the Faculty Senate and on various committees. I want to thank Bill Lyne, in Western's English Department, who, as the first president of our faculty union, urged me to write for the union's blog, providing me with an outlet to test publicly some of my ideas.

My History Department colleagues work tirelessly to help students understand the value of a liberal education and to experience it. Down the hall from me is the Philosophy Department, where Dennis Whitcomb has time and again shared his time and knowledge, especially concerning my queries about the intellectual virtues.

I want to end by thanking my partner, Kate Destler. She has encouraged me consistently and has also been a critical reader. Her doubts have forced me to think again and then again about what I am trying to say. An expert in education policy, she often knows more than I do. She does not like simple explanations, especially when she knows that the truth is subtle. I am deeply grateful for her willingness to read and reread, to push me when necessary, and to help me make my argument as clear and effective as possible.

———————

MOST OF THE CHAPTERS in this book started out as occasional essays written over the past decade. They have all been revised and updated for this volume. I want to acknowledge their original publication and thank the publishers for permission to reuse this material.

Preface: "College Degrees or College Education,"
    Hedgehog Review (blog), (Sept. 17, 2015).
Introduction: "Making Sense of the Higher Education
    Debate," *Inside Higher Ed* (Sept. 6, 2013).
Chapter 1: "Let's Not Rush into Disruptive Innovation,"
    Inside Higher Ed (Mar. 16, 2017).
Chapter 2: "A Tale of Two Newmans," *Inside Higher Ed*
    (Feb. 16, 2016), and "Margaret Spellings's Vision for
    Higher Education," *Inside Higher Ed* (Oct. 27, 2015).
Chapter 3: "For-Profits' War on Philanthropy," *Inside
    Higher Ed* (Apr. 26, 2012).
Chapter 4: "The Arts and Sciences, or STEM?,"
    WISCAPE blog, Wisconsin Center for the
    Advancement of Postsecondary Education,
    University of Wisconsin–Madison (Feb. 23, 2016).

Chapter 5: "From the Humanities to Humanism in an Era of Higher Education Reform?" *Process: A Blog for American History*, Organization of American Historians (Feb. 28, 2017).

Chapter 7: "Time and Money," *Inside Higher Ed* (Jan. 30, 2015); "Experience Matters: Why Competency-Based Education Will Not Undermine Seat Time," *Liberal Education* 99, 04 (2013). Reprinted with permission. Copyright 2013 by the Association of American Colleges & Universities.

Chapter 8: "Online Higher Education's Individualist Fallacy," *Insider Higher Ed* (Oct. 6, 2011).

Chapter 10: "Ministers, not MBAs," *Inside Higher Ed* (Oct. 3, 2014).

Chapter 11: "How to Evaluate Academic Research," *Inside Higher Ed* (May 15, 2014).

Chapter 12: "Coming Down from the Clouds: On Academic Writing," *Chronicle of Higher Education* (Mar. 7, 2016).

Conclusion: "Taking It to the Streets: Preparing for an Academy in Exile," *Liberal Education* 100, 04 (2014). Reprinted with permission. Copyright 2014 by the Association of American Colleges & Universities.

NOTES

PREFACE. *On Education versus Degrees*

1. Barack Obama, quoted in Tal Brewer, "What Good Are the Humanities," *Raritan* 38, 04 (2018), 98–118, at 99. See also Stanley Fish, "Race to the Top of What?" *New York Times Opinionator* (blog), (Jan. 31, 2011), https://opinionator.blogs.nytimes.com/2011/01/31/race-to-the-top-of-what-obama-on-education/. On Obama's comments about art history, see Scott Jaschik, "Obama vs. Art History," *Inside Higher Ed* (Jan. 31, 2014), https://www.inside highered.com/news/2014/01/31/obama-becomes-latest-politician -criticize-liberal-arts-discipline.

2. For example, see Bill Destler, "The President's New Higher Education Agenda," *HuffPost* (Sept. 3, 2013), http://www.huffington post.com/bill-destler/the-presidents-new-higher_b_3860804.html.

3. Susan Dynarski, "New Data Gives Clearer Picture of Student Debt," *New York Times*, online ed. (Sept. 10, 2015), https://www.nytimes.com/2015/09/11/upshot/new-data-gives-clearer-picture -of-student-debt.html?_r=0.

INTRODUCTION. *On the Purpose(s) of College Education*

1. Jeffrey Selingo, *College (Un)Bound: The Future of Higher Education and What It Means for Students* (Boston, 2013), 20.

2. Mark Edmundson, *Why Teach? In Defense of a Real Education* (New York, 2013), 14.

3. James T. Kloppenberg, *Reading Obama: Dreams, Hopes, and the American Political Tradition* (Princeton, NJ, 2010).

4. Ronald Brownstein, "Floodwaters Lift Poverty Debate into Focus," *Los Angeles Times* (Sept. 13, 2005), http://articles.latimes.com/2005/sep/13/nation/na-poverty13.

5. Mary Beth Marklein, "Universities Bolster MOOCs for Online Learning," *USA Today* (May 30, 2013), https://www.usatoday.com/story/news/nation/2013/05/30/universities-coursera-moocs-online-learning/2371421/.

6. Scott Jaschik, "'Shake Up' for Higher Education," *Inside Higher Ed* (July 25, 2013), https://www.insidehighered.com/news/2013/07/25/obama-vows-shake-higher-education-and-find-new-ways-limit-costs; Carl Straumshein and Ry Rivard, "Enjoying White House Attention," *Inside Higher Ed* (Aug. 23, 2013), https://www.insidehighered.com/news/2013/08/23/higher-ed-reformers-obama-speech-was-welcome-attention.

7. Bill Destler, "The President's New Higher Education Agenda," *HuffPost* (Sept. 3, 2013), http://www.huffingtonpost.com/bill-destler/the-presidents-new-higher_b_3860804.html.

8. Kevin Kiley, "A Blunt Instrument," *Inside Higher Ed* (Feb. 14, 2013), https://www.insidehighered.com/news/2013/02/14/white-houses-new-scorecard-oversimplifies-institutions-liberal-arts-advocates-say.

9. Michael Sandel, *Justice: What's the Right Thing to Do?* (New York, 2009); Alasdair MacIntyre, *After Virtue: A Study in Moral Theory* (Notre Dame, IN, 1984).

10. Francis Oakley, *Community of Learning: The American College and the Liberal Arts Tradition* (New York, 1992).

11. Linda Trinkaus Zagzebski, *Virtues of the Mind: An Inquiry into the Nature of Virtue and the Ethical Foundations of Knowledge* (Cambridge, 1996), 126. My goal is not to offer an exhaustive account of the intellectual virtues. For more detailed explorations, see Zagzebski, *Virtues of the Mind*, pt. 2; Jason Baehr, *The Inquiring Mind: On Intellectual Virtues and Virtue Epistemology* (New York, 2011), ch. 2; Ron Ritchart, *Intellectual Character: What It Is, Why It Matters, and How to Get It* (San Francisco, 2002); John Turri, Mark Alfano, and John Greco, "Virtue Epistemology," *The Stanford Encyclopedia of Philosophy*, ed. Edward N. Zalta (Winter 2017 ed.), https://plato.stanford.edu/archives/win2017/entries/

epistemology-virtue/. I have also been informed by Julia Annas, *The Morality of Happiness* (New York, 1993), esp. ch. 2. See also Barry Schwartz and Kenneth Sharpe, "Colleges Should Teach Intellectual Virtues," *Chronicle of Higher Education* (Feb. 19, 2012), http://www .chronicle.com/article/Colleges-Should-Teach/130868/.

12. Johann N. Neem, "A University without Intellectuals: Western Governors University and the Academy's Future," *Thought & Action* (Fall 2012), 62–79, http://www.nea.org/assets/docs/HE/ 2012-TA-Neem.pdf; Claire Goldstein, "The Emergent Academic Proletariat and Its Shortchanged Students," *Dissent* (Aug. 14, 2013), https://www.dissentmagazine.org/online_articles/the-emergent -academic-proletariat-and-its-shortchanged-students.

13. Joseph Raz, *The Practice of Value*, ed. Jay Wallace (New York, 2003), 19.

CHAPTER 1. *On Disruptive Innovation*

1. Clayton M. Christensen and Henry J. Eyring, *The Innovative University: Changing the DNA of Higher Education from the Inside Out* (San Francisco, 2011); Evan Goldstein, "The Undoing of Disruption," *Chronicle Review* (Sept. 15, 2015), http://www.chronicle.com/ article/The-Undoing-of-Disruption/233101.

2. *A Test of Leadership: Charting the Future of U.S. Higher Education*, A Report of the Commission Appointed by Secretary of Education Margaret Spellings (US Department of Education, 2006), http://www2.ed.gov/about/bdscomm/list/hiedfuture/reports/ final-report.pdf.

3. Quoted in Johann N. Neem, "Disruptive Innovation: Rhetoric or Reality?," *Inside Higher Ed* (June 26, 2012), https://www.inside highered.com/views/2012/06/26/disruption-excuse-politically -motivated-changes-essay. See also Derek Quizon, "Dragas' Eight Year Stint on U.Va. Board Ends," *Richmond Times-Dispatch* (June 11, 2016), http://www.richmond.com/news/virginia/dragas-eight-year -stint-on-u-va-board-ends/article_f4260ba4-4e88-544d-aa94 -d142dcaf41d7.html.

4. Paul LeBlanc, "Credit for What You Know, Not for How Long You Sit," *New England Journal of Higher Education*, online ed. (Sept. 10, 2013), http://www.nebhe.org/thejournal/credit-for-what -you-know-not-how-long-you-sit/.

5. Johann N. Neem, "A University without Intellectuals: Western Governors University and the Academy's Future," *Thought & Action* (Fall 2012), 62–79, http://www.nea.org/assets/docs/HE/2012-TA -Neem.pdf.

6. Kirsten Korosec, "Ford's New High Tech Headquarters Will Take a Decade to Build," *Fortune* (Apr. 12, 2016), http://fortune.com/ 2016/04/12/ford-high-tech-headquarters/.

7. Ben Grubb, "Do as We Say, Not as We Do: Googlers Don't Telecommute," *Sydney Morning Herald* (Feb. 19, 2013), http://www .smh.com.au/it-pro/business-it/do-as-we-say-not-as-we-do-googlers -dont-telecommute-20130218-2e08w.

8. Michael M. Crow and William B. Dabars, *Designing the New American University* (Baltimore, 2015), 275.

9. Written Testimony to the Committee on Health, Education, Labor, and Pensions from Paul LeBlanc, President, Southern New Hampshire University (Oct. 2013), http://www.help.senate.gov/imo/ media/doc/LeBlanc.pdf.

10. Hartmut Rosa, "Social Acceleration: Ethical and Political Consequences of a Desynchronized High-Speed Society," in *High-Speed Society: Social Acceleration, Power, and Mobility*, ed. Rosa and William E. Scheuerman (State College, PA, 2008), ch. 6.

11. Crow and Dabars, *Designing the New American University*, 182.

12. Andrew A. King and Baljir Baatartogtokh, "How Useful Is the Theory of Disruptive Innovation?" *MIT Sloan Management Review* 57, 01 (2015), 77–90.

13. Jill Lepore, "The Disruption Machine: What the Gospel of Innovation Got Wrong," *New Yorker* (June 23, 2014), https://www .newyorker.com/magazine/2014/06/23/the-disruption-machine.

14. Maggie Berg and Barbara Seeber, *The Slow Professor: Challenging the Culture of Speed in the Academy* (Toronto, 2016).

15. Daniel F. Chambliss and Christopher G. Takacs, *How College Works* (Cambridge, MA, 2014).

16. Richard Arum and Josipa Roksa, *Academically Adrift: Limited Learning on College Campuses* (Chicago, 2010).

17. Daniel T. Willingham, *Why Don't Students Like School?: A Cognitive Scientist Answers Questions about How the Mind Works and What It Means for the Classroom* (San Francisco, 2009); James E. Zull, *The Art of Changing the Brain* (Sterling, VA, 2002).

CHAPTER 2. *On Two Recent Occasions*

1. Kellie Woodhouse, "Chaos in North Carolina," *Inside Higher Ed* (Oct. 19, 2015), https://www.insidehighered.com/news/2015/10/19/unc-presidential-search-chaos-amid-charges-politicization-and-secrecy.

2. *A Test of Leadership: Charting the Future of U.S. Higher Education*, A Report of the Commission Appointed by Secretary of Education Margaret Spellings (US Department of Education, 2006), http://www2.ed.gov/about/bdscomm/list/hiedfuture/reports/final-report.pdf.

3. Johann N. Neem, "A University without Intellectuals: Western Governors University and the Academy's Future," *Thought & Action* (Fall 2012), 62–79, http://www.nea.org/assets/docs/HE/2012-TA-Neem.pdf.

4. Scott Jaschik, "Reforming the Requirement-Free Curriculum," *Inside Higher Ed* (Sept. 15, 2008), https://www.insidehighered.com/news/2008/09/15/brown.

5. John T. Casteen III, "Governance and Institutional Transformation: Some Lessons Yet to Be Learned," *Liberal Education* 99, 03 (2013), https://www.aacu.org/publications-research/periodicals/governance-and-institutional-transformation-some-lessons-yet-be.

6. David Fleischacker, "The Place of Modern Scientific Research in the University according to John Henry Newman," *Logos: A Journal of Catholic Thought and Culture* 15, 02 (2012), 101–17.

7. John Henry Newman, *The Idea of a University* (1853, 1858; Garden City, NY, 1959).

8. Liz Bowie, "Simon Newman Named Mount St. Mary's President," *Baltimore Sun* (Dec. 8, 2014), http://www.baltimoresun.com/news/maryland/education/blog/bs-md-mount-st-marys-president-20141208-story.html.

9. Scott Jaschik, "Are At-Risk Students Bunnies to Be Drowned?" *Inside Higher Ed* (Jan. 20, 2016), https://www.insidehighered.com/news/2016/01/20/furor-mount-st-marys-over-presidents-alleged-plan-cull-students.

10. Simon Newman, "Mount St. Mary's President Defends His Efforts to Retain Students," *Washington Post* (Jan. 20, 2016),

https://www.washingtonpost.com/news/grade-point/wp/2016/
01/20/mount-st-marys-university-president-defends-his-efforts-to
-retain-students/?utm_term=.f1e6a2a38e27; Will B. Mackintosh,
"The Scorecard Bites Back," online blog post (Feb. 9, 2016), http://
www.willmackintosh.org/history-2/the-scorecard-bites-back/.

11. Rakesh Khurana, *From Higher Aims to Hired Hands: The
Social Transformation of American Business Schools and the Unfulfilled
Promise of Management as a Profession* (Princeton, NJ, 2007).

12. Beryl A. Radin, *Challenging the Performance Movement:
Accountability, Complexity, and Democratic Values* (Washington, DC,
2006).

13. John Schwenkler, "What (Who?) Is a University?," *First
Things* (Feb. 12, 2016), https://www.firstthings.com/web-exclusives/
2016/02/what-who-is-a-university.

14. Scott Jaschik, "Is Controversial President Questioning Catholic Role?," *Inside Higher Ed* (Feb. 12, 2016), https://www.inside
highered.com/news/2016/02/12/controversial-president-mount
-st-marys-accused-undercutting-its-catholic-role.

15. http://msm.university/, as it appeared on Feb. 15, 2016.

16. http://msm.university/learn-here, as it appeared on Feb. 15, 2016.

17. http://msm.university/succeed-anywhere, as it appeared on
Feb. 15, 2016.

18. Susan Svrluga, "Amid National Backlash, Mount St. Mary's
President Defends His Tenure in Letter to Parents," *Washington Post*,
online ed. (Feb. 10, 2016), https://www.washingtonpost.com/news/
grade-point/wp/2016/02/10/in-letter-to-parents-mount-st-marys
-president-defends-his-tenure-amid-national-backlash/?utm_term
=.feod5b126944.

CHAPTER 3. *On For-Profit Schools*

1. Paul Fain, "Santorum Says Obama Is Waging 'War' on
For-Profits," *Inside Higher Ed* (Feb. 22, 2012), https://www.inside
highered.com/quicktakes/2012/02/22/santorum-says-obama-waging
-war-profits; Emma Brown, Valerie Strauss, and Danielle Douglas-
Gabriel, "Trump's First Full Education Budget: Deep Cuts to Public
Schools in Pursuit of School Choice," *Washington Post*, online ed.
(May 17, 2017), https://www.washingtonpost.com/local/education/

trumps-first-full-education-budget-deep-cuts-to-public-school
-programs-in-pursuit-of-school-choice/2017/05/17/2a25a2cc
-3a41-11e7-8854-21f359183e8c_story.html?tid=a_inl&utm_term
=.580d365e5434. For a good overview of the complex social and
economic reasons leading to the rise of for-profit higher education,
see Tressie McMillan Cottom, *Lower Ed: The Troubling Rise of
For-Profit Colleges in the New Economy* (New York, 2017); Suzanne
Mettler, *Degrees of Inequality: How the Politics of Higher Education
Sabotaged the American Dream* (New York, 2014).

2. Olivier Zunz, *Philanthropy in America* (Princeton, NJ, 2012).

3. Johann N. Neem, "Private Wealth, Public Influence," *Common-
Place* 07, 04 (2007), http://www.common-place-archives.org/vol-07/
no-04/talk/.

4. Among many sources, see Sheila Slaughter and Larry L. Leslie,
*Academic Capitalism: Politics, Policies, and the Entrepreneurial Uni-
versity* (Baltimore, 1999).

5. Robert Zemsky, *Making Reform Work: The Case for Transforming American Higher Education* (New Brunswick, NJ, 2009), 105.

6. Senate Committee on Health, Education, Labor, and Pensions,
*For-Profit Higher Education: The Failure to Safeguard the Federal
Investment and Ensure Success* (July 2012), Executive Summary,
http://www.help.senate.gov/imo/media/for_profit_report/Executive
Summary.pdf. See also Cottom, *Lower Ed.*

7. See the discussion of how for-profits use algorithms to target
vulnerable Americans in order to generate profit, in Cathy O'Neil,
*Weapons of Math Destruction: How Big Data Increases Inequality
and Threatens Democracy* (New York, 2016), ch. 4. Studies suggest
that for-profit degrees are not worth the investment. See Stephanie
Riegg Cellini, "Gainfully Employed? New Evidence on the Earnings,
Employment, and Debt of For-Profit Certificate Students," Brown
Center *Chalkboard*, Brookings Institution (Feb. 9, 2018), https://
www.brookings.edu/blog/brown-center-chalkboard/2018/02/09/
gainfully-employed-new-evidence-on-the-earnings-employment
-and-debt-of-for-profit-certificate-students.

8. Michael Sandel, *What Money Can't Buy: The Moral Limits of
Markets* (New York, 2012), esp. 120–22.

9. A concise overview of the economic arguments against for-
profit education can be found in Samuel F. Abrams, *Education and
the Commercial Mindset* (Cambridge, MA, 2016), ch. 8.

10. David J. Deming, Claudia Goldin, and Lawrence F. Katz, "The For-Profit Postsecondary School Sector: Nimble Critters or Agile Predators?," *Journal of Economic Perspectives* 26, 01 (2012), 139–64, http://pubs.aeaweb.org/doi/pdfplus/10.1257/jep.26.1.139.

11. Kevin Kinser, *From Main Street to Wall Street: The Transformation of For-Profit Higher Education* (San Francisco, 2006).

CHAPTER 4. *On STEM*

1. Patricia Cohen, "A Rising Call to Promote STEM Education and Cut Liberal Arts Funding," *New York Times* (Feb. 21, 2016), https://www.nytimes.com/2016/02/22/business/a-rising-call-to-promote-stem-education-and-cut-liberal-arts-funding.html?ref=education&_r=0.

2. See discussion and statistics in Andrew Hacker, *The Math Myth and Other STEM Delusions* (New York, 2016), ch. 3.

3. Kira Hamman, "Why STEM Should Care about the Humanities," *Chronicle of Higher Education*, online ed. (Apr. 12, 2013), http://www.chronicle.com/blogs/conversation/2013/04/12/why-stem-should-care-about-the-humanities/?cid=at&utm_source=at&utm_medium=en.

4. On these points, see also David R. Johnson, *A Fractured Profession: Commercialism and Conflict in Academic Science* (Baltimore, 2017).

5. Andrew Jewett, *Science, Democracy, and the American University: From the Civil War to the Cold War* (New York, 2012).

6. Statistics and quote in Johnson, *A Fractured Profession*, 1–2. See also Eric J. Vettel, *Biotech: The Countercultural Origins of an Industry* (Philadelphia, 2006).

7. On the origins of human capital theory, see Peter Fleming, "What Is Human Capital?," *Aeon* (May 10, 2017), https://aeon.co/essays/how-the-cold-war-led-the-cia-to-promote-human-capital-theory.

CHAPTER 5. *On the Humanities*

1. Paul Kristeller, *Renaissance Thought: The Classic, Scholastic, and Humanist Strains* (New York, 1961), 13. See also Olaf Pedersen, *The First Universities: Studium Generale and the Origins of University*

Education in Europe (Cambridge, 1997), 196–204; Bruce A. Kimball, *Orators & Philosophers: A History of the Idea of Liberal Education* (New York, 1986), 82–87.

2. Anthony Grafton and Lisa Jardine, *From Humanism to the Humanities: Education and the Liberal Arts in Fifteenth- and Sixteenth-Century Europe* (Cambridge, MA, 1986), 197.

3. Kimball, *Orators & Philosophers*, esp. chs. 5–6. For an intriguing discussion of the continued relevance of the ancient debate between knowledge and skills, see Jennifer Summit and Blakey Vermeule, *Action versus Contemplation: Why an Ancient Debate Still Matters* (Chicago, 2018).

4. On the rise of the American research university, see James Axtell, *Wisdom's Workshop: The Rise of the Modern University* (Princeton, NJ, 2016); Roger Geiger, *The History of American Higher Education: Learning and Culture from the Founding to World War II* (Princeton, NJ, 2015); John R. Thelin, *A History of American Higher Education* (Baltimore, 2004).

5. Laurence Veysey, *The Emergence of the American University* (Chicago, 1965).

6. Jürgen Herbst, *The Once and Future School: 350 Years of American Secondary Education* (New York, 1996).

7. Robert Middlekauff, *Ancients and Axioms: Secondary Education in Eighteenth-Century New England* (New Haven, CT, 1963).

8. I make this argument in Johann N. Neem, *Democracy's Schools: The Rise of Public Education in America* (Baltimore, 2017), esp. chs. 1–2.

9. James Turner, *Philology: The Forgotten Origins of the Modern Humanities* (Princeton, NJ, 2014). See also Jaap Maat, "The *Artes Sermocinales* in Times of Adversity: How Grammar, Logic, and Rhetoric Survived the Seventeenth Century," in *The Making of the Humanities*, vol. 1, *Early Modern Europe*, ed. Rens Bod, Jaap Maat, and Thijs Weststeijn (Amsterdam, 2010), 283–94.

10. Peter Novick, *That Noble Dream: The "Objectivity" Question and the American Historical Profession* (New York, 1988).

11. Daniel Coit Gilman, "The Utility of Universities," (1885), reprinted in *The Rise of the Research University: A Sourcebook*, ed. Louis Menand, Paul Reitter, and Chad Wellmon (Chicago, 2017), 170–86.

12. In addition to Turner's *Philology,* see Julie A. Reuben, *The Making of the Modern University: Intellectual Transformation and the Marginalization of Morality* (Chicago, 1996), ch. 7;

W. B. Carnochan, *The Battleground of the Curriculum: Liberal Education and the American Experience* (Stanford, CA, 1993).

13. Woodrow Wilson, "Princeton for the Nation's Service" (1902), http://infoshare1.princeton.edu/libraries/firestone/rbsc/mudd/online_ex/wilsonline/4dn8nsvc.html.

14. Geoffrey Galt Harpham, *The Humanities and the Dream of America* (Chicago, 2011), 17.

15. *General Education in a Free Society: Report of the Harvard Committee* (Cambridge, MA, 1945), 51, 59, 64. See Christopher Loss, *Between Citizens and the State: The Politics of American Higher Education in the 20th Century* (Princeton, NJ, 2012).

16. Michael Meranze, "Humanities out of Joint," *American Historical Review* 120, 04 (2015), 1311–26; Ellen Schrecker, *The Lost Soul of Higher Education: Corporatization, the Assault on Academic Freedom, and the End of the American University* (New York, 2010).

17. Harpham, *Humanities and the Dream of America*, ch. 6; Meranze, "Humanities out of Joint," 1322–26.

18. See, for example, Kevin Dougherty, "Mass Higher Education: What Is Its Impetus? What Is Its Impact?" *Teachers College Record* 99, 01 (1997), 66–72; Victor E. Ferrall, *Liberal Arts at the Brink* (Cambridge, MA, 2011), esp. ch. 3. The classic discussion of the emergence of the mass university remains Martin Trow, "Problems in the Transition from Elite to Mass Higher Education," reprinted in *Twentieth-Century Higher Education: Elite to Mass to Universal*, ed. Michael Burrage (Baltimore, 2010), 88–142.

19. Christopher Newfield, *The Great Mistake: How We Wrecked Public Universities and How We Can Fix Them* (Baltimore, 2016).

20. Scott Cohen, "The Boutique Liberal Arts?" *Liberal Education* 100, 04 (2014), https://www.aacu.org/liberaleducation/2014/fall/cohen.

21. Johann N. Neem, "The Common Core and Democratic Education," *Hedgehog Review* 17, 02 (2015), http://www.iasc-culture.org/THR/THR_article_2015_Summer_Neem.php; Thomas D. Fallace, *In the Shadow of Authoritarianism: American Education in the Twentieth Century* (New York, 2018).

22. On these points, see Russell Muirhead, *Just Work* (Cambridge, MA, 2004).

23. Wendy Brown, *Undoing the Demos: Neoliberalism's Stealth Revolution* (New York, 2015), 177–78, 181.

CHAPTER 6. *On Business Majors*

1. National Center for Education Statistics, "Digest of Education Statistics," 2011 Tables and Figures, table 286, https://nces.ed.gov/programs/digest/d11/tables/dt11_286.asp (accessed June 25, 2018).

2. Bill Destler, "The President's New Higher Education Agenda," *HuffPost* (Sept. 3, 2013), http://www.huffingtonpost.com/bill-destler/the-presidents-new-higher_b_3860804.html.

3. Willard Dix, "It's Time to Worry When Colleges Erase Humanities Departments," *Forbes* (Mar. 15, 2018), https://www.forbes.com/sites/willarddix/2018/03/13/its-time-to-worry-when-colleges-erase-humanities-departments/#.

4. The University of Texas "Seek UT" website was accessed on Apr. 9, 2018. See https://seekut.utsystem.edu/.

5. Anthony Carnevale et al., *What's It Worth? The Economic Value of College Majors*. A Report of the Georgetown University Center on Education and the Workforce (Washington, DC), https://cew.georgetown.edu/wp-content/uploads/2014/11/whatsitworth-select.pdf.

6. American Academy of Arts & Sciences Humanities Indicators, "Earnings of Humanities Majors with a Terminal Bachelor's Degree" (Feb. 2018), https://www.humanitiesindicators.org/content/indicatorDoc.aspx?i=64.

7. "Pay for Liberal-Arts Graduates vs. Professional and Pre-professional Graduates, by Age Group, 2012," *Chronicle of Higher Education's Almanac of Higher Education* (2014), http://www.chronicle.com/article/Pay-for-Liberal-Arts-Graduates/147311/.

8. Jeff Guo, "Want Proof College Is Worth It? Look at This List of High-Paying Majors," *Washington Post* (Sept. 24, 2014), https://www.washingtonpost.com/news/storyline/wp/2014/09/29/want-proof-college-is-worth-it-look-at-this-list-of-the-highest-paying-majors/?utm_term=.fa5fa4fcb0cb.

9. AAC&U, "The Economic Case for Liberal Education," 2016 rev. ed., https://www.aacu.org/leap/economiccase.

10. "Salary Increase by Major," *Wall Street Journal*, online ed., http://online.wsj.com/public/resources/documents/info-Degrees_that_Pay_you_Back-sort.html.

11. Benjamin Schmidt, "The Humanities Are in Crisis," *Atlantic*, online ed. (Aug. 23, 2018), https://www.theatlantic.com/education/archive/2018/08/the-humanities-face-a-crisisof-confidence/567565/.

12. American Academy of Arts & Sciences, *The State of the Humanities 2018: Graduates in the Workforce and Beyond* (Cambridge, MA, 2018), 10, 13, 20.

13. George Anders, "That 'Useless' Liberal Arts Degree Has Become Tech's Hottest Ticket," *Fortune*, online ed. (July 29, 2015), https://www.forbes.com/sites/georgeanders/2015/07/29/liberal-arts -degree-tech/#95cc72f745d2.

14. AAC&U, "It Takes More Than a Major" (Apr. 10, 2013), http://www.aacu.org/sites/default/files/files/LEAP/2013_Employer Survey.pdf.

15. John L. McCaffrey, "What Corporation Presidents Think about at Night," *Fortune* (Sept. 1953), 129–29, 140, 142; William Benton, "The Failure of the Business Schools," *Saturday Evening Post* (Feb. 18, 1961), 26, 73–76. Both authors are cited in Steven Conn, *No Success Like Failure: The Sad History of American Business Schools* (forthcoming, Ithaca, NY), ch. 2.

16. Richard Arum and Josipa Roksa, *Academically Adrift: Limited Learning on College Campuses* (Chicago, 2010).

17. Richard Arum and Josipa Roksa, *Aspiring Adults Adrift: Tentative Transitions of College Students* (Chicago, 2014).

18. Fareed Zakaria, book excerpt, "In Defense of a Liberal Education," *ABC News*, online ed. (Mar. 27, 2015), http://abcnews.go.com/ Politics/book-excerpt-defense-liberal-education-fareed-zakaria/story ?id=29901850&singlePage=true. See also Geoffrey Galt Harpham, *What Do You Think, Mr. Ramirez? The American Revolution in Education* (Chicago, 2017).

19. Scott Cohen, "The Boutique Liberal Arts?" *Liberal Education* 100, 04 (2014), https://www.aacu.org/liberaleducation/2014/fall/ cohen.

20. Barry Schwartz, "What 'Learning How to Think' Really Means," *Chronicle of Higher Education Review*, online ed. (June 28, 2015), http://www.chronicle.com/article/What-Learning-How-to-Think/ 230965/.

21. Talbot Brewer, "The Coup That Failed: How the Near-Sacking of a University President Exposed the Fault Lines of American Higher Education," *Hedgehog Review* 16, 02 (2014), http://iasc -culture.org/THR/THR_article_2014_Summer_Brewer.php.

22. Frederick Wherry, *The Culture of Markets* (Malden, MA, 2012).

23. On this point, see Conn, *No Success Like Failure.*

24. William Deresiewicz, "Don't Send Your Kids to the Ivy League," *New Republic* (July 21, 2014), https://newrepublic.com/article/118747/ivy-league-schools-are-overrated-send-your-kids-elsewhere.

25. B. D. McClay, "With Friends Like These," *THR Blog* (June 28, 2015), http://iasc-culture.org/THR/channels/THR/2015/06/with-friends-like-these/.

26. Cathie Gandel, "Business Schools Give Undergraduate Education a Liberal Arts Twist," *U.S. News & World Report*, online ed. (Sept. 9, 2015), https://www.usnews.com/education/best-colleges/articles/2015/09/09/business-schools-give-undergraduate-programs-a-liberal-arts-twist. This is also why advocates of liberal education cannot be reassured by David Labaree's recent argument that American professional programs, in order to raise their prestige and rankings, have emulated the arts and sciences by favoring abstract thought over practical skills and by putting important liberal content into their programs. Labaree concludes that the academicization of professional training, spurred by student-consumers' demand for prestige, means that American professional programs proclaim professional or vocational ends while relying on liberal content. There is much truth to this, but, as Labaree admits,

> at one level, we have liberal content masquerading as professional education, where the practicality of the education rides on its ability to land you a job rather than to teach you vocational skills. But at another level, we have a system that offers students little inducement to learn this liberal content, because their attention is focused on what they can buy with their educational credentials rather than how they can apply their knowledge.

And that is precisely the problem. Even when professional programs embrace the content of the liberal arts and sciences, they orient their students away from the ends of liberal education, including the cultivation of intellectual virtues. See David Labaree, *A Perfect Mess: The Unlikely Ascendency of American Higher Education* (Chicago, 2017), ch. 4: "Mutual Subversion: The Liberal and the Professional," quote at 93.

27. William Major, "Close Business Schools, Save the Humanities," *Inside Higher Ed* (July 28, 2014), https://www.insidehighered.com/views/2014/07/28/essay-calling-new-perspective-business-schools-and-humanities. See also Conn, *No Success Like Failure*.

CHAPTER 7. *On Time and Experience*

1. Arne Duncan, "Beyond the Iron Triangle: Containing the Cost of College and Student Debt." Remarks of US Secretary of Education Arne Duncan to the annual Federal Student Aid Conference, Las Vegas, Nov. 29, 2011, http://www.ed.gov/news/speeches/beyond-iron-triangle-containing-cost-college-and-student-debt; Barack Obama, White House Office of the Press Secretary, 2013, "FACT SHEET on the President's Plan to Make College More Affordable: A Better Bargain for the Middle Class," White House, August 22, http://www.whitehouse.gov/the-press-office/2013/08/22/fact-sheet-president-s-plan-make-college-more-affordable-better-bargain-.

2. Jared Cameron Bass, Amy Latinen, and Clare McCann, "The Department of Deregulation: DeVos's New Regulatory Agenda to Roll Back Protections for Students," *New America Foundation* (blog), (Mar. 30, 2018), https://www.newamerica.org/education-policy/edcentral/the-department-of-deregulation/; Kelly Field, "Student Aid Can Be Awarded for 'Competencies,' Not Just Credit Hours, U.S. Says." *Chronicle of Higher Education* (Mar. 19, 2013), http://www.chronicle.com/article/Student-Aid-Can-Be-Awarded-for/137991.

3. Ed Ayers, "The Experience of Liberal Education," *Liberal Education* 96, 03 (2010), 6–11.

4. Gary Gutting, "Why Do I Teach?," *New York Times Opinionator* (blog), (May 22, 2013), http://opinionator.blogs.nytimes.com/2013/05/22/why-do-i-teach/?hp.

5. Thomas Friedman, "How to Get a Job," *New York Times* (May 28, 2013), http://www.nytimes.com/2013/05/29/opinion/friedman-how-to-get-a-job.html.

6. Daniel T. Willingham, *Why Don't Students Like School?: A Cognitive Scientist Answers Questions about How the Mind Works and What It Means for the Classroom* (San Francisco, 2009); James E. Zull, *The Art of Changing the Brain* (Sterling, VA, 2002).

7. Lawrence Cremin, *American Education*, 3 vols. (New York, 1970–80).

8. American Historical Association, *History Discipline Core: American Historical Association Tuning Project* (Washington, DC, 2012), http://www.historians.org/projects/tuning/HistoryDiscipline CoreInitial%20Release_08-28-12.pdf.

9. According to Linda Trinkaus Zagzebski, *Virtues of the Mind: An Inquiry into the Nature of Virtue and the Ethical Foundations of Knowledge* (Cambridge, 1996, 116), "it takes time to develop virtues and vices, and this feature is connected with the fact that we hold persons responsible for these traits. Once a virtue or vice develops, it becomes entrenched in a person's character and becomes a kind of second nature." In other words, we need to offer students sufficient time to develop their intellectual virtues so that seeking intellectual understanding becomes habitual and internalized. If we speed up the time to a college degree too much, students will not have enough time to develop their intellectual virtues.

10. Michael Oakeshott, "A Place of Learning," (1975), in Oakeshott, *The Voice of Liberal Learning* (Indianapolis, IN, 2001), 1–34.

11. Daniel F. Chambliss and Christopher G. Takacs, *How College Works* (Cambridge, MA, 2014).

12. Willingham, *Why Don't Students Like School?*

CHAPTER 8. *On Online Education*

1. For a good overview, see Anthony G. Picciano, *Online Education Policy and Practice: The Past, Present, and Future of the Digital University* (New York, 2017).

2. Ezra Klein, "It's a Hard-Knock Life," *Washington Post*, online ed. (Oct. 18, 2010), http://voices.washingtonpost.com/ezra-klein/2010/10/its_a_hard-knock_life.html.

3. Richard Vedder, "Cheap, Maybe Even Free, Higher Education," *Chronicle of Higher Education*, online ed. (Sept. 27, 2011), http://www.chronicle.com/blogs/innovations/cheap-maybe-even-free-higher-education/30348; Anya Kamenetz, *DIY U: Edupunks, Edupreneurs, and the Coming Transformation of Higher Education* (White River Junction, VT, 2010); Jeffrey R. Young, "Bill Gates Predicts Technology Will Make 'Place-Based' Colleges Less Important in 5 Years," *Chronicle of Higher Education* (Aug. 9, 2010), https://www.chronicle.com/blogs/wiredcampus/bill-gates-predicts-technology-will-make-place-based-colleges-less-important-in-5-years/26092.

4. Quotes and examples from Michael Fabricant and Stephen Brier, "Technology as a 'Magic Bullet' in an Era of Austerity," in *Austerity Blues: Fighting for the Soul of Public Higher Education* (Baltimore, 2016), ch. 6.

5. Richard Arum and Josipa Roksa, *Academically Adrift: Limited Learning on College Campuses* (Chicago, 2010).

6. Jaron Lanier, *You Are Not a Gadget: A Manifesto* (New York, 2010).

7. Danielle Allen et al., *Education and Equality* (Chicago, 2016).

8. Daniel T. Willingham, *Why Don't Students Like School? A Cognitive Scientist Answers Questions about How the Mind Works and What It Means for Your Classroom* (San Francisco, 2009).

9. Parker Palmer, *The Courage to Teach: Exploring the Inner Landscape of a Teacher's Life*, 3d ed. (San Francisco, 1998), 10–11.

10. Tamar Lewin, "Online Enterprises Gain Foothold as Path to a College Degree," *New York Times* (Aug. 25, 2011), http://www.nytimes.com/2011/08/25/education/25future.html?_r=1.

CHAPTER 9. *On Critical Thinking*

1. Richard Arum and Josipa Roksa, *Academically Adrift: Limited Learning on College Campuses* (Chicago, 2010); Nicholas Lemann, "The Case for a New Kind of Core," *Chronicle of Higher Education* (Nov. 27, 2016), https://www.chronicle.com/article/The-Case-for-a-New-Kind-of/238479. For an overview of the rise of the "critical thinking" movement, see William T. Gormley Jr., *The Critical Advantage: Developing Critical Thinking Skills in School* (Cambridge, MA, 2017), ch. 1.

2. Thomas L. Friedman, "How to Get a Job," *New York Times* (May 28, 2013), http://www.nytimes.com/2013/05/29/opinion/friedman-how-to-get-a-job.html.

3. Steven C. Ward, "The Competency-Based Approach to Higher Education: Are the AAC&U and Other Organizations Destroying Liberal Traditions?" *Thought & Action* (Summer 2016).

4. I raise this question in Johann N. Neem, "Does History Matter? A Cautionary Tale for the Tuning Project," *Perspectives on History* (Apr. 2013).

5. See Nicholas Tampio, *Common Core: National Education Standards and the Threat to Democracy* (Baltimore, 2018); Johann N. Neem, "The Common Core and Democratic Education," *Hedgehog Review* 17, 02 (2015), 102–10, https://iasc-culture.org/THR/THR_article_2015_Summer_Neem.php.

6. Johann N. Neem, "Skills Don't Matter (Outside Their Context),"

Inside Higher Ed (Feb. 23, 2018), https://www.insidehighered.com/views/2018/02/23/skills-disconnected-academic-programs-shouldnt-matter-colleges-opinion. See also David Labaree, "The Five-Paragraph Fetish," *Aeon* (Feb. 15, 2018), https://aeon.co/essays/writing-essays-by-formula-teaches-students-how-to-not-think.

7. As Jason Baehr, *The Inquiring Mind: On Intellectual Virtues and Virtue Epistemology* (New York, 2011), 30–31, argues, skills are distinct from intellectual virtues: "Imagine, for instance, a person who is disposed to engage in careful and thorough scientific research, but whose ultimate concern lies strictly with professional status or a potential financial payoff. Such a person would not be good or better qua person on account of these traits." Baehr continues: "An intellectually virtuous person necessarily chooses or pursues the object of her virtue (e.g. knowledge or understanding) for its own sake, but that a person with various intellectual skills (skills with the same intentional object) might be motivated substantially or even entirely by other ends." See also Linda Trinkaus Zagzebski, *Virtues of the Mind: An Inquiry into the Nature of Virtue and the Ethical Foundations of Knowledge* (Cambridge, 1996), 106–16; Harvey Siegel, "Critical Thinking and the Intellectual Virtues," in *Intellectual Virtues and Education: Essays in Applied Virtue and Epistemology*, ed. Jason Baehr (New York, 2016), ch. 6.

8. Molly Worthen, "The Misguided Drive to Measure 'Learning Outcomes,'" *New York Times* (Feb. 23, 2018), https://www.nytimes.com/2018/02/23/opinion/sunday/colleges-measure-learning-outcomes.html.

9. This deeper conception of critical thinking is offered in Gormley, *The Critical Advantage*, ch. 2; Lemann, "A New Kind of Core." For a thorough discussion, see James Turner, *Philology: The Forgotten Origins of the Modern Humanities* (Princeton, NJ, 2014).

10. Video: Harvard-Smithsonian Center for Astrophysics, "A Private Universe" (1987), Annenberg Learner, https://www.learner.org/resources/series28.html#.

11. E. D. Hirsch Jr., *Why Knowledge Matters: Rescuing our Children from Failed Educational Theories* (Cambridge, MA, 2016), 81–87.

12. Hirsch, *Why Knowledge Matters*, ch. 7, argues that test scores decline when schools emphasize skills over content. This explains some of what happened in the United States, but more dramatically

and recently in France and Sweden. As a result, if American colleges were to focus on skills, as recent reformers advocate, instead of the subject matter taught by the arts and sciences, they might produce worse outcomes.

13. Andrew Hacker, *The Math Myth and Other STEM Delusions* (New York, 2016), ch. 6, esp. 82–86.

14. K. Anders Ericsson, ed., *The Cambridge Handbook of Expertise and Expert Performance* (New York, 2006); Hirsch, *Why Knowledge Matters*.

15. Daniel T. Willingham, *The Reading Mind: A Cognitive Approach to Understanding How the Mind Reads* (San Francisco, 2017), esp. chs. 4–6, quote at 135; Daniel T. Willingham and Gail Lovette, "Can Reading Comprehension Be Taught?" *Teachers College Record* (Sept. 26, 2014); Daniel T. Willingham, "How Knowledge Helps," *American Educator* (Spring 2006), https://www.aft.org/periodical/american-educator/spring-2006/how-knowledge-helps.

16. Harvard University, *General Education in a Free Society: Report of the Harvard Committee* (Cambridge, MA, 1945).

17. On the latter point, see Johann N. Neem, "Funding Students, Threatening Liberal Education," *Inside Higher Ed* (Dec. 20, 2011), https://www.insidehighered.com/views/2011/12/20/essay-washington-college-grant-program-favors-vocational-over-liberal-education.

18. For strategies on effective teaching to help students learn the material more effectively, see Peter C. Brown, Henry L. Roediger III, and Mark A. McDaniel, *Make It Stick: The Science of Successful Learning* (Cambridge, MA, 2014); James E. Zull, *The Art of Changing the Brain* (Sterling, VA, 2002).

19. Hirsch, *Why Knowledge Matters*, ch. 1. The MLK example is taken from a comment by David Coleman, one of the primary authors of the Common Core, who encouraged teachers to teach MLK without providing context. See discussion in Thomas D. Fallace, Johann N. Neem, and Fritz Fischer, "Is the Common Core a Threat to History Education?" *American Historian* (Nov. 2015), 10–14; Tampio, *Common Core*, ch. 3. See also Sam Wineburg, *Why Learn History (When It's Already on Your Phone)* (Chicago, 2018), chs. 4, 5; Jessica Lahey, "To Read Dickens, It Helps to Know French History and the Bible," *Atlantic Monthly*, online ed. (Jan. 27, 2014), https://www.theatlantic.com/education/archive/2014/01/to-read-dickens-it-helps-to-know-french-history-and-the-bible/283346/.

20. Thomas Jefferson, *Notes on the State of Virginia*, Query XIV, in *Thomas Jefferson: Writings*, ed. Merrill D. Peterson (New York, 1984), 271–75.

21. Chester E. Finn Jr., "Emphasis on Thinking Skills over Facts in Schools Contributes to Truth Decay," *EducationNext* (Jan. 26, 2018), http://educationnext.org/emphasis-thinking-skills-facts-schools -contributes-truth-decay/. The study referred to is Jennifer Kavanagh and Michael D. Rich, "Truth Decay: An Initial Exploration of the Diminishing Role of Facts and Analysis in American Public Life" (Rand Corporation, 2018), https://www.rand.org/pubs/research _reports/RR2314.html.

CHAPTER 10. *On the PhD*

1. Vimal Patel, "Proposal to Offer Job-Friendly English Ph.D. Draws Criticism," *Chronicle of Higher Education*, online ed. (Sept. 15, 2014), https://www.chronicle.com/article/Proposal-to-Offer-Job -Friendly/148779; Modern Language Association Task Force on Doctoral Study in Modern Language and Literature, "Report of the MLA Task Force on Doctoral Study in Modern Language and Literature" (2014), http://www.mla.org/pdf/taskforcedocstudy2014.pdf.

2. Anthony Grafton and James Grossman, "No More Plan B: A Very Modest Proposal for Graduate Programs in History," *Perspectives on History* (Oct. 2011), https://www.historians.org/ publications-and-directories/perspectives-on-history/october-2011/ no-more-plan-b.

3. Elizabeth Segran, "What Can You Do with a Humanities PhD, Anyway?," *Atlantic* (Mar. 31, 2014), https://www.theatlantic.com/ business/archive/2014/03/what-can-you-do-with-a-humanities-phd -anyway/359927/.

4. Leonard Cassuto, *The Graduate School Mess: What Caused It and How We Can Fix It* (Cambridge, MA, 2015), 1–2.

5. Richard Harris, "Too Few University Jobs for America's Young Scientists," NPR's *Morning Edition* (Sept. 16, 2014), https://www .npr.org/sections/health-shots/2014/09/16/343539024/too-few -university-jobs-for-americas-young-scientists.

6. Jesse Lemisch, "A WPA for History: Occupy the American Historical Association," *New Politics*, online ed. (Jan. 24. 2012),

http://newpol.org/content/wpa-history-occupy-american
-historical-association.

7. Marc Bousquet, "The Waste Product of Graduate Education: Toward a Dictatorship of the Flexible," *Works and Days* 41/42, vol. 21, nos. 1–2 (2003), http://www.worksanddays.net/2003/ File09.Bousquet_File09.Bousquet.pdf.

8. Stephen Mucher, "The Liberal Arts Role in Teacher Education," *Inside Higher Ed* (July 17, 2014), https://www.insidehighered .com/views/2014/07/17/liberal-arts-faculty-need-get-more -involved-teacher-education-essay.

9. Robert B. Townsend, *History's Babel: Scholarship, Professionalization, and the Historical Enterprise in the United States, 1880–1940* (Chicago, 2013).

10. William L. Duren Jr., "Afterthoughts on College Education" (unpublished), http://www.wldurenjrmemorial.net/writings.html.

11. Harvard Divinity School Program, https://hds.harvard.edu/ academics/degree-programs/mdiv-program/mdiv-requirements. Accessed Apr. 18, 2018.

12. Princeton Theological Seminary, "Master of Divinity," https://pt sem.edu/academics/degrees/master-of-divinity. Accessed Sept. 24, 2018.

13. Cassuto, *The Graduate School Mess*, 144–50.

CHAPTER 11. *On Research*

1. Tracy Jan, "GOP Pushes Funding Cuts for Social Science Work," *Boston Globe* (Apr. 14, 2014); Michael Stratford, "Higher Ed Cuts in GOP Budget," *Inside Higher Ed* (Apr. 2, 2014), https://www .insidehighered.com/news/2014/04/02/ryan-budget-calls-cuts-pell -grant-elimination-neh#sthash.RL5hD1kc.dpbs.

2. Nicholas Kristof, "Professors, We Need You!," *New York Times* (Feb. 15, 2014), https://www.nytimes.com/2014/02/16/opinion/ sunday/kristof-professors-we-need-you.html; Corey Robin, "Look Who Kristof's Saving Now," blog post (Feb. 16, 2014), http://corey robin.com/2014/02/16/look-who-nick-kristofs-saving-now/.

3. Paula A. Michaels, "What Is Academic History For?" *Oxford University Press OUP Blog* (Mar. 29, 2014), https://blog.oup.com/ 2014/03/what-is-academic-history-for/.

4. Jocelyn Kaiser, "NIH Details Impact of 2013 Sequester Cuts,"

Science, online ed. (May 8, 2013), http://www.sciencemag.org/news/2013/05/nih-details-impact-2013-sequester-cuts; William J. Broad, "Billionaires with Big Ideas Are Privatizing American Science," *New York Times* (Mar. 15, 2014), https://www.nytimes.com/2014/03/16/science/billionaires-with-big-ideas-are-privatizing-american-science.html.

5. Johann N. Neem, "The Value of Useless Research," *Academe Blog* (Nov. 28, 2011), https://academeblog.org/2011/11/28/the-value-of-useless-research/.

6. On this point, see Rens Bod, *A New History of the Humanities: The Search for Principles and Patterns from Antiquity to the Present* (Oxford, 2014), 14–20, 353–54.

7. Obergefell v. Hodges, 135 S. Ct. 2584 (2015).

8. Nancy F. Cott, *Public Vows: A History of Marriage and the Nation* (Cambridge, MA, 2000); Hendrik Hartog, *Man and Wife in America: A History* (Cambridge, MA, 2000); Stephanie Coontz, *Marriage, a History: From Obedience to Intimacy; or, How Love Conquered Marriage* (New York, 2005).

9. Michael Meranze, "Curating the Humanities," *Remaking the University*, blog post (Nov. 28, 2013), http://utotherescue.blogspot.com/2013/11/curating-humanities.html; "Scott Walker's Effort to Weaken College Tenure," *New York Times* (June 5, 2015), https://www.nytimes.com/2015/06/06/opinion/scott-walkers-effort-to-weaken-college-tenure.html.

10. Walter Isaacson, *The Innovators: How a Group of Hackers, Geniuses, and Geeks Created the Digital Revolution* (New York, 2014).

CHAPTER 12. *On Academic Writing*

1. Dennis Overbye, "Gravitational Waves Detected, Confirming Einstein's Theory," *New York Times* (Feb. 11, 2016).

2. Steven Pinker, "Why Academics Stink at Writing," *Chronicle of Higher Education Review* (Sept. 26, 2014), https://www.chronicle.com/article/Why-Academics-Writing-Stinks/148989.

3. Naomi Wolf and Sacha Kopp, "Should Academics Talk to Katie Couric?" *Chronicle of Higher Education*, online ed. (Feb. 17, 2016), https://www.chronicle.com/article/Should-Academics-Talk-to-Katie/235341.

4. Wolf and Kopp, "Should Academics Talk to Katie Couric?"

5. Victoria Clayton, "The Needless Complexity of Academic Writing," *Atlantic* (Oct. 26, 2015), https://www.theatlantic.com/education/archive/2015/10/complex-academic-writing/412255/.

6. James Baldwin, "The White Man's Guilt," *Ebony* (Aug. 1965).

7. Ernest Renan, reprinted in *Becoming National: A Reader*, ed. Geoff Eley and Ronald Grigor Suny (New York, 1996), 42–55.

8. Cicero, *On the Ideal Orator*, trans. James May and Jakob Wise (New York, 2001).

9. Peter Drier, "Academic Drivel Report," *American Prospect*, online ed. (Feb. 22, 2016), http://prospect.org/article/academic-drivel-report.

10. Lawrence M. Krauss, "Finding Beauty in the Darkness," *New York Times* (Feb. 11, 2016).

CONCLUSION. *On the Future*

1. Randall Stross, *A Practical Education: Why Liberal Arts Graduates Make Great Employees* (Stanford, CA, 2017); Claudia Goldin and Lawrence F. Katz, *The Race between Education and Technology* (Cambridge, MA, 2008); Tim Marshall, "STEM May Be the Future, but Liberal Arts Are Timeless," *Quartz* (Feb. 27, 2018), https://qz.com/1215910/stem-may-be-the-future-but-liberal-arts-are-timeless/.

2. Laurence Veysey, *The Emergence of the American University* (Chicago, 1965); David Labaree, *A Perfect Mess: The Unlikely Ascendancy of American Higher Education* (Chicago, 2017).

3. Geoffrey Galt Harpham, *What Do You Think, Mr. Ramirez? The American Revolution in Education* (Chicago, 2017); Julie Reuben, *The Making of the Modern University: Intellectual Transformation and the Marginalization of Morality* (Chicago, 1996).

4. Ronald Reagan, "Radio Address to the Nation on the Federal Role in Scientific Research" (Apr. 2, 1988), http://www.presidency.ucsb.edu/ws/?pid=35637.

5. This point is made most baldly by Bryan Callahan, *The Case against Education: Why the Education System Is a Waste of Time and Money* (Princeton, NJ, 2018). It should be clear that I disagree with much of what Callahan argues. In particular, I disagree that

the benefits of education should be primarily economic. But he raises an important question that advocates of education cannot ignore: What is the social cost of demanding that more people receive college degrees when they neither want to study college subjects, nor is it clear that the degree is useful other than as a signal of employability? My answer is that we need to emphasize the importance of the education, not the degree.

6. On this latter point, see Charles T. Clotfelter, *Unequal Colleges in the Age of Disparity* (Cambridge, MA, 2017); Sara Goldrick-Rab, *Paying the Price: College Costs, Financial Aid, and the Betrayal of the American Dream* (Chicago, 2016); Suzanne Mettler, *Degrees of Inequality: How the Politics of Higher Education Sabotaged the American Dream* (New York, 2014).

7. Christopher Newfield, *The Great Mistake: How We Wrecked Public Universities and How We Can Fix Them* (Baltimore, 2016); Dylan Matthews, "The Tuition Is Too Damn High: 3 Reasons Why Tuition Is Rising," *Washington Post* (Aug. 28, 2013), http://www .washingtonpost.com/blogs/wonkblog/wp/2013/08/28/the-tuition -is-too-damn-high-part-iii-the-three-reasons-tuition-is-rising/; Karin Fischer and Jack Stripling, "An Era of Neglect," *Chronicle of Higher Education* (Mar. 2, 2014), https://www.chronicle.com/ article/An-Era-of-Neglect/145045?cid=at&utm_source=at&utm _medium=en&elqTrackId=afcea32fc357446581f9866d45c6c5ea &elq=754a96dc432d4804833adbf139c109ce&elqaid=17983&elqat =1&elqCampaignId=7980.

8. Newfield, *The Great Mistake*; Ellen Schrecker, "'Tough Choices': The Changing Structure of Higher Education," in *The Lost Soul of Higher Education: Corporatization, the Assault on Academic Freedom, and the End of the American University* (New York, 2010), ch. 6.

9. Chad Wellmon, "Whatever Happened to General Education?" *Hedgehog Review* 19, 01 (2017), http://iasc-culture.org/THR/THR _article_2017_Spring_Wellmon.php.

10. Hans-Georg Tiede, *University Reform: The Founding of the American Association of University Professors* (Baltimore, 2015); Benjamin Ginsberg, *The Fall of the Faculty and the Rise of the All-Administrative University and Why It Matters* (New York, 2011).

11. Frank Donoghue, *The Last Professors: The Corporate University and the Fate of the Humanities* (New York, 2008); A. J. Angulo, "From Golden Era to Gig Economy: Changing Contexts

for Academic Labor in America," in *Professors in the Gig Economy: Unionizing Adjunct Faculty in America*, ed. Kim Tolley (Baltimore, 2018), 3–26.

12. See American Academy of Arts and Sciences, *The Heart of the Matter: The Humanities and Social Sciences for a Vibrant, Competitive, and Secure Nation* (Cambridge, MA, 2013), http://www .humanitiescommission.org/_pdf/hss_report.pdf.

13. David Hollinger, quoted in Robin Wilson, "Humanities Scholars See Declining Prestige, Not a Lack of Interest," *Chronicle of Higher Education* (July 15, 2013), http://chronicle.com/article/ Humanities-Scholars-See/140311/.

14. Michael Meranze, "Curating the Humanities," *Remaking the University* (blog), (Nov. 28, 2013), http://utotherescue.blogspot .com/2013/11/curating-humanities.html.

15. See "Humanities by the Numbers," *AAC&U News* (Aug. 2013), http://archive.aacu.org/aacu_news/aacunews13/August13/facts _figures.cfm; Nate Silver, "As More Attend College, Majors Become More Career Focused," *Five Thirty Eight* (blog), *New York Times* (June 25, 2013), https://fivethirtyeight.blogs.nytimes.com/2013/06/ 25/as-more-attend-college-majors-become-more-career-focused/; American Academy of Arts & Sciences, "Humanities Indicators," http://www.humanitiesindicators.org/content/hrcoIIA.aspx#topII1; Michael Bérubé, "The Humanities Declining? Not according to the Numbers," *Chronicle of Higher Education Review* (July 25, 2013), http://chronicle.com/article/The-Humanities-Declining-Not/140093/.

16. Benjamin Schmidt, "The Humanities Are in Crisis," *Atlantic*, online ed. (Aug. 23, 2018), https://www.theatlantic.com/education/ archive/2018/08/the-humanities-face-a-crisisof-confidence/567565/.

17. Kevin Dougherty, "Mass Higher Education: What Is Its Impetus? What Is Its Impact?" *Teachers College Record* 99, 01 (1997), 66–72; Martin Trow, "Problems in the Transition from Elite to Mass Higher Education," reprinted in *Twentieth-Century Higher Education: Elite to Mass to Universal*, ed. Michael Burrage (Baltimore, 2010), 88–142.

18. I draw the shopping mall analogy from Arthur G. Powell, *The Shopping Mall High School: Winners and Losers in the Educational Marketplace* (Boston, 1985).

19. Clark Kerr, *The Uses of the University*, 3rd ed. (Cambridge, MA, 1982), 1, 41.

20. Andrew Sullivan, "Journalism's Surrender," *The Dish* (blog), (Dec. 31, 2013), http://dish.andrewsullivan.com/2013/12/31/journalisms-surrender.

21. Sandeep Jauhar, "Shouldn't Doctors Control Hospital Care?" *New York Times*, online ed. (Oct. 10, 2017), https://www.nytimes.com/2017/10/10/opinion/shouldnt-doctors-control-hospital-care.html?action=click&pgtype=Homepage&clickSource=story-heading&module=opinion-c-col-right-region&region=opinion-c-col-right-region&WT.nav=opinion-c-col-right-region&_r=0; Marcia Angell, "Drug Companies and Doctors: A Story of Corruption," *New York Review of Books* (Jan. 15, 2009), http://www.nybooks.com/.

22. Adam Smith, *The Wealth of Nations* (Indianapolis, IN, 1976). See also George Leef, "The Spirit of Adam Smith Returns," *Commentaries* blog, John William Pope Center for Higher Education Policy (Feb. 12, 2013), http://www.popecenter.org/commentaries/article.html?id=2805; John Paul Rollert, "What Adam Smith Can Teach Us about Incentives in Higher Education," *Boston Review* (blog), (Nov. 4, 2013), http://www.bostonreview.net/blog/rollert-adam-smith-education-incentives.

23. Katharine Destler, "Creating a Performance Culture: Incentives, Climate, and Organizational Change," *American Review of Public Administration* 46, 02 (2016), 201–25; William Firestone, "Teacher Evaluation Policies and Conflicting Theories of Motivation," *Educational Researcher* 43, 02 (2014): 100–107.

24. John R. Thelin and Richard W. Trollinger, *Philanthropy and American Higher Education* (New York, 2014); Olivier Zunz, *Philanthropy in America: A History* (Princeton, NJ, 2012), 8–43.

25. Marjorie Pryse, "Artisanal Teaching," *Chronicle of Higher Education Review* (Aug. 5, 2013), http://chronicle.com/article/Artisanal-Teaching/140611?cid=megamenu; Scott L. Newstok, "A Plea for 'Close Learning,'" *Liberal Education* 99, 04 (2013), http://www.aacu.org/liberaleducation/le-fa13/newstok.cfm.

26. David Reid, "Education as a Philanthropic Enterprise: The Dissenting Academies of 18th-Century Britain," *History of Education* 39, 03 (2010): 299–317; Matthew Mercer, "Dissenting Academies and the Education of the Laity, 1750–1850," *History of Education* 30, 01 (2001): 35–58; H. McLachlan, *English Education under the Test Acts: Being the History of Non-conformist Academies, 1662–1800*

(Manchester, UK, 1931). For the American context, see Jürgen Herbst, *From Crisis to Crisis: American College Government, 1636–1819* (Cambridge, MA, 1982).

27. This would also require challenging the assumption that, among nonmedical academic disciplines, only psychology can help people think about how they orient their lives. Academics from other disciplines would have to demonstrate that the humanities, the social sciences, and the natural sciences have much to teach people of all ages about their place in the world and what it means to live a meaningful life.

28. Dorinda Outram, *The Enlightenment* (Cambridge, 1995), 14–30; Alexandra Oleson and Sanborn C. Brown, eds., *The Pursuit of Knowledge in the Early American Republic: American Scientific and Learned Societies from Colonial Times to the Civil War* (Baltimore, 1976).

29. Joseph F. Kett, *The Pursuit of Knowledge under Difficulties: From Self-Improvement to Adult Education in America, 1750–1990* (Stanford, CA, 1994). For an inspiring story of one institution committed to adult liberal education, see Anya Kamenetz, "This College for Adult Learners Is a Refuge, Not Just a Career Boost," *NPR*, online ed. (July 4, 2018), https://www.npr.org/sections/ed/2018/07/04/616778773/this-college-for-adult-learners-is-a-refuge-not-just-a-career-boost.

30. The phrase is from Francis Oakley, *Community of Learning: The American College and the Liberal Arts Tradition* (New York, 1992).

INDEX